THE
RICHARD STILGOE
LETTERS

A
JUMBLE
OF
ANAGRAMS

This book
is
dedicated
to

AGNES BELLANOTI
ALISON A. BENTLEG
ALLIE T. SONGBANE
ELIA SLAGBONNET
ELENA O'BLASTING
ENA I. LOST-BANGLE
and
ANGELA SNOB-TILE

who are my wife

THE
RICHARD STILGOE
LETTERS

A JUMBLE OF ANAGRAMS

**With cartoons
by
RICHARD WILLSON**

London
GEORGE ALLEN & UNWIN
Boston   Sydney

First published in 1981

GEORGE ALLEN & UNWIN LTD
40 Museum Street, London WC1A 1LU

Text © Richard Stilgoe, 1981
Illustrations © Richard Willson, 1981

British Library Cataloguing in Publication Data

Stilgoe, Richard
  The Richard Stilgoe Letters.
  1. English wit and humor
  I. Title
  828'.91409   PN6175

  ISBN 0-04-827035-0

Designed
by
Maynard & Jefferis Publishing
28-32 Shelton Street, London WC2

Phototypeset in Plantin medium by
Carlinpoint Ltd.

Printed and bound in Great Britain by
Biddles Ltd, Guildford and King's Lynn

CONTENTS

PREFACE

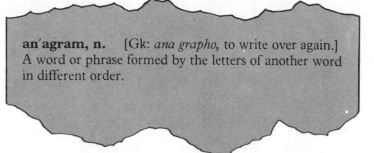

an'agram, n. [Gk: *ana grapho*, to write over again.] A word or phrase formed by the letters of another word in different order.

YEARS AGO, WHILE fooling about with a set of Scrabble letters, I made a wonderful discovery: from the letters that make up the word ORCHESTRA you can create the word CARTHORSE. And, of course, vice versa. I remember being delighted by this happy coincidence, since the two things have so much in common. An orchestra, like a carthorse, is large and powerful and has a tendency to go its own way at its own pace unless attended by a man with a stick. The coincidence seemed almost mystical, as though those nine letters imposed a character on whatever they formed.

In the middle ages, the Christian scholars and the Rabbis firmly believed this and spent much time doing anagrams of the scriptures in order to find deeper meanings. Thus Pilate, when he says QUID EST VERITAS? (What is truth?), is producing an anagram of EST VIR QUI ADEST (It is the man before you) and this people thought very meaningful.

Elizabeth I, a superstitious old bat at the best of times, was given to asking her astrologer, Doctor Dee (1527-1608. Well researched, isn't it! He's buried in Mortlake) for advice. "Doctor," she would say, "I would lie with the Earl of Essex. What manner of luxurie will he bring to my bed?" And Doctor Dee would make the THE EARL OF ESSEX with his Scrabble set, jumble it about and produce

HE FERES SEX A LOT (note Tudor spelling). So Elizabeth I would lose interest.

But *some* of the coincidences in the anagram world really are quite uncanny. During the Crimean war the Victorians might have worked out that FLORENCE NIGHTINGALE was an anagram of FLIT ON CHEERING ANGEL—and of CLING ON FEELING HEART. They could have added TEN FACING GORE IN HELL (from the missing verse of *The Charge of the Light Brigade:* "Ten facing gore in Hell, Didn't the boys do well? Noble six hundred") or perhaps G.C.E. FRONTLINE HEALNG, the exam Florence Nightingale had to pass to get out to the Crimea and issue such commands as "LEG ON FIRE—CHANGE LINT" or the peremptory "FETCH NIGEL AN IRON LEG". Coincidence, yes. Serendipity, yes. But from the same set of letters we can get T. HALL ENGINEERING CO., RINGO THE CLEANING ELF and NEIL THE GINGER FALCON, none of whom have the remotest conection with nursing or the Crimean War. For those letters—A, O, C, F, H, R, T, two I's, G's, L's, three E's and three N's can be arranged over two thousand million different ways.

'An orchestra, like a carthorse, is large and powerful and has a tendency to go its own way at its own pace unless attended by a man with a stick.'

ALL CREATURES BRIGHT AND BEAUTIFUL

"GRISTDALE, 5¾ MILES. Unsuitable for motor vehicles," said the sign. Cheerfully, CHRIS DOGTAILER turned the Austin Ruby (which he'd never thought of as a motor vehicle, more as a trusted friend and ally) towards the direction pointed by the wooden finger.

Ever since, as a boy, he'd first read *All The Fun Of The Fur* and *Pussies Galore*, he'd sworn that he too would be a friendly Yorkshire vet and have hilarious and heart-warming adventures. His parents had warned him off: "There's no brass in monkeys, son," his father said. Chris's resolve remained unshaken. Finally, he gave his parents a copy of *Distemper On My Ceiling* and one night, when ITV was on strike, his father read it. Next morning Chris noticed a change in him, a softening, but it wasn't for three weeks that he discovered the magnitude of that change. As Chris returned from evening classes one night, his father was waiting on the doorstep. He was waving a letter. "You got it, Chris. You got it," he called.

What, wondered Chris as he walked up the path, had he got? Measles? He asked his father.

"Why, the job of course," said his father.

"What job, Daddy?" asked Chris.

His father looked sheepish. "I never told you," he said. "Slipped my mind." And he explained.

Distemper On My Ceiling had moved him greatly. Knowing Chris's desire to emulate its author, he had decided to help. Seeing an advertisement for a vacancy in a Yorkshire practice, he had applied on Chris's behalf, adding that Chris, though as yet unqualified, had a nice smile and several tweed jackets. The letter he was waving was the reply. "They want you up there tomorrow," said his father, and he read the letter aloud:

> *Never mind about the qualifications, as long as you can fire a humane killer you're our man. Look forward to meeting you.*
>
> *Yours sincerely,*
>
> *Wotan Roberts*

"There. Funny name, Wotan. Foreign, I dare say."

"It's Wagner," said Chris.

"Really," said his father. "Looks like Wotan to me. Probably pronounced Wagner, I dare say."

All this raced through Chris's mind (well, not raced—it wasn't that sort of mind—more ambled) as he drove over the dales towards Gristdale. He was still pondering his good fortune as he knocked on the door of IRISCHART LODGE, a stone house as neat as a new pin, but bigger. The door was opened halfway by a bluff, red-faced man carrying a bow and arrows. "Yes," he barked. "Who the hell are you?"

"I'm Chris Dogtailer, sir, your new assistant."

"Of course, of course. Come in, then. Don't just stand there."

Chris went in, pushing the door fully open. A large bag of flour fell on his head, bursting as it did so.

The laughter from Wotan Roberts (for it was he) went on for some minutes, growing when a younger version of Wotan walked into the room and saw Chris lying in a floury heap, his nice smile and tweed jacket both the worse for wear. This turned out to be Parsifal, Wotan's younger brother and another cheerful soul. When their laughter died down, they introduced themselves. "Chris Dogtailer," said Chris.

"Bloody silly name," said Parsifal and roared with laughter. Wotan threw the coal-scuttle at him. It caught Parsifal on the side of the head, knocking him down and making him bleed from the

'A large bag of flour fell on his head, bursting as it did so.'

ear. This Wotan appeared to find even funnier than the bag of
flour. Parsifal sufficiently contained his mirth (and the bleeding)
to make a pot of tea.

"Why the bow and arrows?" asked Chris. "If it's not a rude
question."

"It is. Bloody rude question," said Wotan. "Answer it though.
Quieter than a gun. Eh, Parsie?"

Parsifal agreed that a bow and arrows were indeed quieter than a
gun. Before Chris could ask why either should be carried by a vet
when answering his front door, the 'phone rang. Wotan answered
it. "Gristdale 377. Who the hell's that? Oh, God! Not bloody
Rover again! Well of course he's ill. Ought to be put out of his
misery, if you want my opinion. Not a chance today. Up to our
eyes. Might manage next Wednesday. I know it is, but we're very
busy. Well, if he dies, he dies. Not my bloody animal." He
slammed the 'phone down. "Bloody Vicar!" he screamed.
"Bloody Rover. Bloody stupid name for a . . ."

Parsifal interrupted him. "Wotan," he said, "*we* may be too
busy to go and see Rover, but—well, what about—er—Chris?"
And he giggled. And Wotan giggled. Then they laughed. Quite
loudly.

Chris got up. "Where does Rover's owner live?" he asked.
"The vicarage?"

"How did you know that?" asked Wotan amazed.

"You said it was the Vicar on the 'phone," said Chris. "I'll go if
you think it would help. Is it far? Will it take me long?"

"Well," said Parsifal. "It's not far, but it will take you quite a
while."

"How so?" asked Chris.

"While Wotan was doing the flour trick on you I let down your
front tyres."

This admission made Parsifal and Wotan laugh so much that
Chris decided to set off by himself without asking any more
questions. Skirting the pile of flour in the hall, he opened the front
door. The church was clearly visible at the top of the hill, beside a
square Georgian house which Chris guessed must be the vicarage.
He set off, pausing only momentarily to inspect the Austin Ruby,

which now sat disconsolately on its flat front tyres and appeared to have gained a swastika in mauve paint on each door and a very large sow asleep on the back seat. Hilarious, thought Chris.

★ ★ ★

The Vicar opened the vicarage door. "Hello," said Chris, in what he hoped was a heart-warming way. "I'm Chris Dogtailer. The Roberts' new assistant. I've just joined them. They asked me to come and have a look at Rover."

"Come in, come in," said the Vicar. "How kind of you to come so quickly. I'm glad Wotan has taken on some help. He's a charming man, but so busy. Always the gentleman, though not, I fear Rover's best friend. They had a difference of opinion on his last visit."

"Well, if a dog isn't man's best friend, who is?" said Chris, and smiled.

"Our Lord, I should imagine," said the Vicar, with a certain asperity. "And I don't see where dogs come into it. Rover is in here." And he led the way into the kitchen, where coiled in front of the kitchen range was a sixteen-foot reticulated python.

"Our Mr Dogtailer will have met Rover by now," said Parsifal. He giggled and took another long drink from his tankard.

Wotan did the same. "Bloody silly name for a snake," he said.

"Bloody silly name for a vet," said Parsifal. They laughed so much they could hardly drink.

★ ★ ★

"Don't worry," said the Vicar. "He's not poisonous. He's a constrictor."

"What's wrong with him?" squeaked Chris.

"He won't eat. He hasn't eaten for weeks. I didn't worry about it to begin with. He quite often only eats once every three weeks or so. And just as well, with the price of Labradors these days."

"Labradors?"

"Won't touch anything else. I've tried lamb, piglet, even calf. He's lost interest. And he used to have such zest. Such love of life. Would you examine him?" The Vicar really looked quite concerned, which he found surprisingly easy.

"Are you *sure* he's not poisonous?" Chris asked. They hadn't got on to reptiles yet at night school.

"Not a bit. And you mustn't think of snake-bite as poison," said the Vicar, launching happily into his lecture. "Venomous snakes merely inject their prey with pepsin—the very same enzyme you and I and Mary and Joseph have in the stomach for digesting food. The snake is merely starting the digestive process earlier than we do, softening up its food chemically to make it easier to eat. The constricting snake does the same thing physically—softens up the food by crushing it. They're fascinating things, and very loving. Touch him."

Chris held out a nervous hand to the sleeping snake. It felt like a very expensive handbag with a live toast-rack inside it—warm and rippling. "Suppose," he said, "it decides that it's gone off Labrador because what it really wants is vet?" He thought that this, though not perhaps hilarious, would provide an acceptable substitute for his first day.

The Vicar didn't smile. "If for some reason he should attack you, don't struggle. Allow him to coil round you, then unwind him from the tail. He cannot resist. Not the head—he's very strong near the head. The tail. Unwind him from there. And keep cool. They see heat, not light. Anything warm, they are attracted to it. Well, I'll leave you with him." And the Vicar shook hands, his palm icy cold in the hot pink hand Chris offered him.

★ ★ ★

"D'you think," said Parsifal. "That we were a bit fiersh with that young chap? I mean Rover'sh a bloody handful sometimes."

"Bloody rubbish," replied Wotan, knocking out one of his brother's teeth with a friendly paperweight. "Chap's got to have a sense of humour, or he'll never survive. Chuck 'em in the deep end, that's what I say. See what they're made of. Chap might be a terrible bore. Got to find out straight away."

"That's what Rover is," said Parsifal.

"What?" said his brother.

"A terrible boa!"

This made them laugh even more. And more still. And by the time Chris, back at the vicarage, finally gave up trying to remember whether it was the tail or the head with which he should begin to unwind the coils of snake which surrounded him, Wotan and Parsifal's laughter had turned to near-hysterical tears.

TREBLE AT T'MILL

IT IS NOT just as the home of Chris Dogtailer, the lovable TV vet, that Gristdale is famous. It is not even for its mill—though it was Gristdale which gave the world the expression "all grist to the mill" in the days when the entire population of the town worked within its stone walls. No, Gristdale's fame in the world is based mainly on the reputation of the GRISTDALE CHOIR of thirty-nine Yorkshire tenors, baritones and basses whose singing has stirred so many hearts and moistened so many eyes.

The choir was founded in 1952 by SIR I. GRADECLOTH (and who, saddled with the first name Ichabod, would not confine himself to an initial whenever possible?) A keen music lover, and a parlour singer of no small ability, he combed the area around Gristdale for singers working at rival mills. Sometimes he would travel as much as twenty miles to persuade a particularly deep bass to move to a rent-free cottage on his estate. One tenor with a folder of certificates from the Huddersfield Festival held out for (and got) an Austin A40 and a radiogram before he signed on at Gristdale.

Though fanatical about choral singing, Sir I. Gradecloth was first a businessman. "Every time that shuttle stops," he would say, "the world is stealing bread from my children." So rehearsal time at the Gristdale Mill was confined to the forty-five-minute dinner break. To begin with, this hampered the choir's performance. Then their choirmaster, ELGAR I. CHORDIST, had a brainwave. During the dinner-break they would rehearse the quiet verses (those needing a concentration which only relative freedom from external noise permitted) but the loud bits—openings, crescendos and climaxes—they would rehearse at the looms during production. This worked splendidly, once a system was worked out for putting the verses into their correct order in performance, since often the choir had rehearsed verses 1, 3 and 5 (the loud ones) in the morning, 2, 4 and half of 6 in the dinner break (2, 4 and half

*'Then their choirmaster had a brainwave.
During the dinnerbreak they would
rehearse the quiet verses.'*

of 6 were all quiet, half of 6 being almost whispered), and the last half of 6 in the afternoon against the clatter of the looms.

All Mr Chordist did was go through the copies, marking loud verses *pp* (production practice) and the quiet ones *fff* (food forty-five). In this way no mistake was possible, though to make doubly sure, many extra copies were printed and at competitive festivals the choir would substitute their spare copies in their rivals' music cases, causing the opposition to sing "All in the April evening" at the tops of their voices.

In this way the Gristdale Choir has won many cups, plaques and plated items—and enough of a reputation for its grateful founder to pay each year for an annual treat, a treat of which they sing the following words at their concerts:

EVERY YEAR WE GO AND SEE THE MOUSETRAP
As sung by the Gristdale Choir

ppp Since 1952 the Gristdale Choir has sung in chorus,
And once a year our secretary organises for us
A coach trip down to London, to go and see a show;
You'll want to know where we all go.

Ev'ry year we go and see *The Mousetrap*.
Since the first night there hasn't been a single year
    we've missed.
It's not queer to go and see *The Mousetrap*
Though the cast all look at us as though we're round
    the twist.

SOLO: One year I broke away from them and went off
    to see *Evita*,
    Afterwards found the West End dark and misty.
TENORS: Misty!
BASSES: Misty!
SOLO: I got lost in the night and missed the coach home.
dim ALL: Serves you right
For being unfaithful to Agatha Christie.

fff Since 1952 we've all been true to just one thriller.
People may say, "How can you, now you've found out
    who's the killer?"
You may think that's the case—I'll tell you
    it's not true,
cres Though we've been since 'fifty-two, we haven't got a clue.

pp Though every year we go and see *The Mousetrap*,
And every year anticipation's every bit as keen,
We've no idea who did it in *The Mousetrap*—
None of us has ever stayed
Awake until the final scene.

HUGHIE GREEN WAS MY VALET

GWILLYM AP RUTHIN stood in the drizzle and gazed at the new grey buildings: slate, Welsh slate, just as the prospectus had shown it. The whole university was clad in brand-new Welsh slate and he, Gwillym ap Ruthin, was its first student on the first day of its first term. The first student at COLEG IDRIS HART, the first university at which all teaching was to be done in Welsh. There's historic.

He had dreamt of this day. His father had dreamt of this day. Many was the time his father had told him the story of Idris Hart, martyr to the Welsh language, the story that had been written down in the university prospectus. The story of how Idris, many years ago, had set out to find food for his family, and had slain a male red deer with a well-aimed lump of coal. He had, with some effort, picked up the hart and started for home. The hart was heavy and Idris was only scrum-half-sized. Soon Idris began to wish he was bringing home a less ostentatious prize.

Then a cart drew up beside him on the road. "Want a hand with the hart?" asked its driver, in the hated English language. (He was an English cat-dealer who made regular forays into the principality with the raw materials for harp strings).

Idris refused to answer. Heavy or not, the deer was not going to get him to admit he understood English, let alone spoke it. The cart carried on.

Six more times Idris was asked, by six different Englishmen, if he wanted help to carry his hart. Six times they got no answer.

Two days later his body was found lying beneath that of the hart. Its skeleton had been picked clean by dogs and boar. The Englishmen all remembered him. It was explained to them that

Idris detested all things English, and never responded when English was spoken to him. He had been willing to die for his Welshness—and indeed to take his family with him, since his failure to return home with something to eat caused their eventual demise as well. So Idris became the symbol of those who fought for the Welsh language, and they called him Idris Hart—mockingly adding the English word that Idris had refused to recognise, the word that had killed him.

That had been 683 years ago. Now Gwillym ap Ruthin, passionate disciple of Idris Hart (he even walked out of Max Boyce concerts after "Sospan Fach" was over and Max lapsed into English), was the first student on the first day of the first term at Coleg Idris Hart. Not to read Welsh. Oh no. That wouldn't have been the point. He was to read *Electronics* in Welsh. *That* was the point—to prove the language was alive and of today.

Exalted, he walked in through the grey slate arch, and into the doorway of the porter's lodge. There was a parcel with his name on in the pigeonhole marked 'R'. He opened the parcel. It was a textbook, with a message in Welsh: "Thought you'd like to see this. First technological textbook in the language. See you at lectures. Ll ap P."

Gwillym seized the book and ran into the quadrangle. He sat on the modernistic slate bench and opened the book. What a triumph! There they all were, the chapter headings—all in Welsh. Microchyps. Transistwrs. Ossylatwrs. Synthysaiswrs. . .

IDI LOSTCHARGER

Ah'm tinkin' Uganda was pretty dam' lucky
To hab such a ruler as me—
Fieldy-marshal, life-peer, Archy-bishop an' sir
An' star ob de screen an' Tee-Vee.
Ah'd go back an' show dem jus' who is still boss
Wid an exipidition'ry force,
But Ah'm stuck wid-out transport like
Richard de Turd—
Won't somebody len' me a horse?

The Dark Continent

A desert sandpit
(President Sadat)

I sing in a hotel band
(Ndabaningi Sithole)

Oops! Ah rule Zimbabwe
(Bishop Abel Muzorewa)

A GRAPPLE A DAY

AS HE WALKED towards the ring, Karate Dave Phipps could hear the cheering already dying away. He broke into a trot, hoping to make it to his corner before the applause stopped altogether. He only just failed. He took off the dressing gown his mum had made him, and a couple of the stuck-on letters fluttered to the canvas: "rate Dave Phipps" it now said on the back, but few people did. He had no glamour, no style. His manager said so. Dave had got quite angry when he said it, and had banged his fist on the manager's desk. The manager had made him buy a new one. For the word "Karate" was no idle addition. Dave Phipps had hands and feet edged with flesh the consistency of a sand-filled sock—as if someone had slipped lead piping under his skin. He could split planks, tiles and bricks, and even open long-life milk cartons. The trouble was that with this skill, he had also imbibed the philosophy of restraint that karate preaches. He was virtually incapable of using his skills in anger. So his wrestling career spiralled downwards, as the weapons that could have brought him stardom hung untested by his sides.

Tonight, however, at least he was fighting a star. Karate Dave could see him now, coming out of the dressing room. The crowd cheered, the band played and the stars and stripes waved above his head as ARLO RIGIDCHEST, heavyweight champion of North America, trundled down the aisle.

"Ladies and gennlemen, our finaller contester isser a catchweighter contester over six roundser. One fall, one submissioner, or ayer knockouter to decider the winner. In the blue corner frommer Catforder at niner stoner seven poundser, Karate Daver Phillips."

Not bothering to correct the M.C. about his name, Dave duly made a Japanese noise and bisected with the side of his hand the brick his second held out for him. There was a smattering of applause.

"Ander inner the redder corner, frommer the Uniteder States ovver America, the North Americaner Heavyweighter Championer, atter twenty-three stoner twelver poundser, Arloer Rigiderchester!"

The crowd erupted, the band played and the meat mountain that was Arlo Rigidchest climbed into the ring. He stood easily six and a half feet tall, and removed his stars and stripes hooded robe to reveal a great oiled barrel of a man, bald and hairless (apart from his chest, the hair of which had been cut to the shape of an American Eagle). He walked around the ring, smiling arrogant acknowledgement of the cheers. Reaching Karate Dave's corner, and continuing to smile, he bent down and picked up half of Dave's demonstration brick. He looked at it, tossed it into the middle of the ring and then, as if it had been a cigarette end, put a foot on the brick and ground it to dust. His second rushed forward with a red, white and blue broom and swept the red molecules of brick from the ring. The crowd roared, nearly drowning the bell which announced the contest's beginning.

Karate Dave Phipps, his hands held out like two ping-pong bats, advanced towards the smiling mountain. With little hope of success, he jabbed upwards at Arlo's navel. The expression on the giant's face changed, and the smile became tinged with regret. The American took hold of the arm pointing to his middle, swung Dave off the ground, executed a couple of circles with him and threw him out of the ring on to the commentator's table.

This was the nearest Dave had ever got to meeting the commentator face to face, and he would have relished the moment had the pain in his back been less severe. He heard the commentator saying, "This looks like the end of the line for Karate Dave Phipps. . . Karate Dave. . . Karate. . ." The red mist of anger carried the word to Dave's brain. Why should he suffer like this, when his hands and feet were as hard as diamonds? The Dave Phipps that returned to the ring as the count reached eight had no thoughts of Japanese philosophy. Spinning twice, he leapt for the American's neck, slashing sideways with the blade of gristle on his right hand. There was a noise as of a cabbage being cut in two. The smiling head of Arlo Rigidchest bounced to the canvas and rolled into a corner.

Dave looked at it and then at the referee, who was considering issuing a public warning. As the three figures stood dumbstruck in the ring, the headless body began to topple and fell forward—with Karate Dave Phipps caught beneath it. The referee, his dilemma solved, counted from one to ten. The crowd cheered, the band played, and in one corner the head of the victorious North American Heavyweight Champion lay on its side and smiled.

Sport

I hang on and rattle
(The Grand National)

A cod made cox hit a Brentford barge
(The Oxford and Cambridge Boat Race)

CRANKSHAFT!
The Magazine for Men

P.O. Box 19, Milton Keynes, Beds.

Mr Charles Gotrigid
The White House
69 Letsby Avenue
Hampton, Middlesex

Dear Charles

You're one of the very first people we've
written to about Crankshaft, the new magazine
for men who believe that thinking is just as
important as doing. We know you'll want to
hear more, because we've been fortunate
enough to send previous publications of ours
to your charming home in Letsby Avenue...

The mixture's as before Charles, the way you
and thousands of other red-blooded commercial
gentlemen say you like it. Our proprietor,
SIGI L.T. HARDCORE, is too canny a bloke to
change the formula that made Rubber Futures,
Bum Steer, Great Tits, Water Bed Storms,
Positions Available and Lay-by such popular
and vital magazines in the past. Once again
our gossip columnist, OLGA DIRTRICHES, will be
telling you who's having who and how. Sexual
problems will be dealt with by our independent
team of advisers, GERDA H. CLITORIS and SERGIO
HARDCLIT. And our tradition of fearless and
relevant reporting isn't forgotten either,
Charles. Issue number one will contain an
investigation into the scandalous doings of

continued.../

the escort agencies run by EDITH O'CARGIRLS
and CATHIE DORGIRLS with full addresses and
telephone numbers.

And the girls haven't been forgotten. We know
that you in .Hampton.. appreciate a curve or two,
so we've sent our photographer, OSCAR I. REDLIGHT,
Stateside, and he's come back with a wow of a
feature he calls 'American Sexdress? That'll do
nicely' in which Yankee Doodles SADIE TORCHGIRL
and CAROL TIGERDISH turn each other into a mass
of stars and stripes, while revealing themselves
in fifty different states.

Well, .Charles, by now you'll be clipping the
coupon and mailing us your £35 for a year's
supply of Crankshaft under plain wrapper. I
know you will. Because if you don't, Crankshaft
will arrive next week at your home in .Letsby..
Avenue.... with no wrapper at all, addressed
personally to you,.Charles, with a pretty hot
picture of one of our Crankshaft grinders on
the cover.

Don't want to have to explain that to
Mrs Gotrigid..., do you .Charles..?

Be hearing from you.

Yours very sincerely,

Chas. Girl-Editor

CHAS. GIRL-EDITOR

SIR RICO THE GLAD
SIR GARTH DOCILE
AND
SIR CLAIR THE DOG

A TIME THERE was, long gone but not yet dead,
When 'neath the crown sat brave King Arthur's head
And in the souls of young men in the realm
There rang the sound of halberd struck on helm,
Of arrow piercing leather, mace through brain,
Of Lancelot panting with the fair Elaine.
But some there were who were not into mail,
Preferring questing for the Holy Grail.
One such, who chose this more ascetic path
Lived in South Cadbury. His name was Garth.
A rude hut shared he there with Ted (his frog),
Morgan the Gerbil and a great big dog,
Full five feet tall with grey and wiry hair,
An ugly beast whom Garth had christened Clair.
Five days a week young Garth with Clair would roam
(The gerbil and the frog stayed back at home)
And by now they were getting pretty sure
The Grail was not in their house or next door,
So one day Garth said, "Clair, we have to face
The fact that it is in some other place—
In number eight, perhaps, or someone's bin;
Or even worse, it could be hidden in
Another street entirely, or worse still,
Its hiding place may be beyond the hill,
Where dragons breathing fire to smoke do dwell
And tax-inspectors too, so I've heard tell."

The dog called Clair just sat while Garth spoke thus
And wondered why his master made such fuss
For dogs, as creatures soulless, mean and lowly,
Do not grasp the importance of things holy,
But while Garth kept on feeding him twice daily,
He'd happily dig holes and look for graily
Antiques therein, though doubtful whether he
Would know one if it bit him on the knee.
The next day Garth gave long instructions verbal
To Ted the frog, likewise Morgan the Gerbil,
On how to run the house while he and Clair
Went on their quest to—well, he knew not where.
And Ted and Morgan nodded and both swore
To leave the milk crate outside the back door,
To add to each week's wash a little softener,
And hoover twice a day or even oftener.

So Garth and Clair the Dog set out to see
What terrors and what wonders there might be

Beyond the hill whose green and rounded brow
Had bounded their experience till now.
They topped it and amazedly did find
A vale just like the one they'd left behind;
No witches, gnomes, or devils, let alone
A dragon—a completely smokeless zone
They saw, and so with confidence they marched
Down to the stream where Clair, whose throat was
        parched,
Stopped and drank for ages from the rill
(Remember, there was lots of him to fill).
An hour or so went by, then noticed Garth
A figure dark approaching on the path,
A little man in suit as black as night.
His shirt was black as well, but brilliant white
His tie was; Signor Rico was his name,
Arthurian protection was his game.
He'd spotted Clair and Garth from far away
And, since things had been pretty quiet today,
He'd charge a fee for letting them across.
(For, truth be told, he usually made a loss.
In Camelot, as folk now would expect,
The peasants didn't have much to protect
And for one who extorted for a living
Rico was far too generous and forgiving.
Tenants of his who got behind with rent
Were never given bootees of cement
But offered loans to help to pay the rental
At interest rates unusually gentle.)
So when he cried, "Hey, you, give me a groat
Or else face down in yonder stream you'll float,"
No malice meant he—it is just the way
Protectionists wish people a good day.
But Garth, a green young country boy, knew not
That this was normal; he just knew he'd got
No groat or penny (times were rather hard,
And this was long before the Barclaycard).

And so, being with terror unacquainted,
Right there and then beside the stream, he fainted.
Rico at this with pangs of guilt was filled—
What if he'd hit his poor head and been killed?
Over the stream he leapt (it wasn't wide,
Since Clair had now got most of it inside).
He knelt down by the body of the boy:
"He isn't dead, he's breathing—joy, oh joy—
But he's not well, a doctor he must see.
I know a man, once trained as an M.D.,
Who specialises now as a magician.
This Merlin holds at court a high position:
Whether by medicine or by magic, he
Must help this fainted youth, and thus help me.
However, he's unconscious—I cannot
Drag him along the ground to Camelot."
'Twas then that Rico noticed standing there,
Still drinking dry the stream, the great dog, Clair,
Who made no move when Garth—just like a sack—
By Rico lifted was on to Clair's back.
Thus Rico, Garth and Clair procession made
To where the court of Arthur was arrayed,
Where Merlin, with a potent magic spell
Once more made Garth red-cheeked and fit and well.
King Arthur then demanded of the youth,
"Tell now the tale (and make sure it's the truth)
Of how you came to Camelot by dog.
Come on, speak up—you must have kept a log."
So Garth explained about the Holy Grail
And how he'd looked at home to no avail,
Had set out on his quest, come to the stream—
And then he said, "I'm sorry I can't seem
To bring the rest to mind. I just passed out."
Then Rico said, "The rest I know about.
A criminal am I, I now confess,
I frightened him and told him that unless
He paid me money I would do him in.

'And so, being with terror unacquainted,
Right there and then beside the stream he fainted.'

I'm sorry, and I realise my sin.
In mitigation can I simply say,
At least I brought him here to you today.
And though you may well lock me up tonight
I'm glad I brought him here and did what's right."
Said Arthur, "Calm your fears—you are no thief.
Come, in the table round put in a leaf!
Many a knight has done things far more bad,
Therefore I dub you SIR RICO THE GLAD.
As to young Garth, for all his quiet docility
He too we elevate to the nobility."
Then with a sword, and with a kingly smile,
He knighted him: "Arise, SIR GARTH DOCILE.
But stay, we will not let it stop at these—
'Tis often said that things turn up in threes.
The hound in all this was a vital cog
And so I say, Arise, SIR CLAIR THE DOG."
The other knights all cheered and toasts were quaffed,
Sir Clair he wagged his tail, and they all laughed.
Sir Garth then thanked the King for all his grace,
And said he ought to go back to his place.
He therefore on Sir Clair's back climbed once more,
And headed the big dog towards the door.
"Hang on," said good King Arthur, "wait a mo—
There's something I have for you ere you go.
Bring in the charger!" Then came in the hall
A white horse fully seventeen hands tall.
" 'Tis yours," said Arthur. "Take it as a gift.'
I'm sorry it's so high. D'you want a lift?"
"Your Majesty," Sir Garth said, "is too kind.
I just hope that Sir Clair the Dog won't mind:
When I by good Sir Rico's threat was shaken
'Twas good Sir Clair who really saved my bacon."
"Marry, and that is true," King Arthur said,
And reached to stroke the great dog's wiry head.
"But folk," said Arthur, "would think it amiss
To send a knight out on a dog like this!"

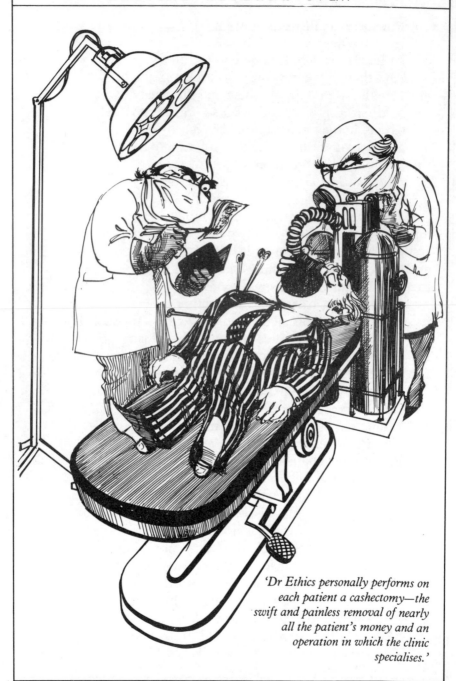

'Dr Ethics personally performs on each patient a cashectomy—the swift and painless removal of nearly all the patient's money and an operation in which the clinic specialises.'

RADICAL ALTERNATIVE MEDICINE

YOU CAN WAIT for months for the operation. Or you can pay through the nose—or whichever organ is affected—and have the operation tomorrow week. Or you can die. These are what medical people refer to as "alternative forms of therapy".

Because more and more people opt for the second, usually by joining private health insurance schemes like BUPA (Brass Usually Prevents Agony) or PPP (Pay to Postpone Pain), more and more private hospitals spring up like unexplained tumours on the tissue of the National Health. Many of these clinics embrace not only conventional medicine, but what we in the West call fringe medicine—things like acupuncture. (If you live in China, acupuncture is regarded as absolutely central to medicine, and the fringe areas are such outrageous treatments as mustard baths or putting your head under a towel and breathing in steam.)

It is just such a clinic that we visit today, a converted mock-German schloss, built in yellow brick in 1897 near High Wycombe, now the property of DR GLORIA ETHICS, a lady doctor of great beauty and much charm and polish, though she is in fact not Polish but Rumanian. Her English accent is virtually perfect, with the merest hint of Rumanian remaining. To Dr Ethics' clinic come the prosperous but poorly from all over the country, to be hit with twigs, drenched in cold water and fed with organic things. After this Dr Ethics personally performs on each patient a cashectomy—the swift and painless removal of nearly all the patient's money, and an operation in which the clinic specialises.

Many are the complaints brought to Dr Ethics' notice: RIGID LARCHTOES, RHODIAC GRISTLE, GASTRIC HELROID and SERGICAL THROID. But most common, perhaps, is ARTHRICOID LEGS. If you take your arthricoid legs along to the National Health Service, they will smile at you exhaustedly and explain that the waiting list for leg replacement is currently five years and even then there is no guarantee that at the point when a bed becomes vacant, a suitable leg will also be available. Leg donors are hard to come by at the best of times, since legs are often damaged in the course of the fatal accident the budding donor has to undergo. And many potential donors have to be turned down when post-mortem examination shows that the very reason they failed to avoid the marauding car was the fact that their legs had themselves become arthricoid.

At Dr Gloria Ethics' clinic, however, no such problems exist. For £6,000 per leg, you're in there next Thursday, your legs are whipped off, and by the Wednesday afterwards you're walking through the front gate feeling a new person. In truth, you only have to reach down and touch your pain-free knees and you *are* feeling a new person. Is £6,000 so much for this? Surely not, when you consider just what is involved. Let's follow a typical arthricoid leg patient from his arrival on Thursday to his departure the next Wednesday. We will call our patient George. His name is in fact Leslie, but he wishes to remain anonymous.

Leslie (sorry, George) arrived at Cutham station on a grey day, with a grey face—a legacy of an indoor working life and legs which were never free from pain. They were long legs, for George is unusually tall (most arthricoid leg sufferers are) and they carried him unsteadily through the station building to the taxi rank. There was one taxi—a red Datsun driven by a fat man in a shiny brown leather jacket which made him look not unlike a conker.

"D'you want to put the case in the boot?"

"Thank you," said George.

"No trouble," said the taxi-driver. "It's not locked."

George, with some effort, lifted his suitcase over the lip of the boot, then climbed into the back seat.

"Bineshaft Court, is it?" asked the taxi-driver, and George agreed. "Thought it must be, the way you was walking," said the taxi-driver, and started his engine. They moved off, with the plastic skeleton twitching happily under the rear-view mirror.

★ ★ ★

The reeded glass of the modern front door of Bineshaft Court

contrasts unhappily with the yellow and white glazed brick around it. The whole house is, indeed, a succession of unhappy contrasts, its combination of towers, battlements, minarets and Dutch gables—all in yellow glazed brick—making it look like a mad pumping station with jaundice. The estate agents had described it as "imposing" and had indicated its unsuitability for human habitation by describing its accommodation in thousands of square feet rather than in numbers of rooms.

But inside the architectural nightmare was the calm influence of Dr Gloria Ethics, who now greeted George with a cool dry hand and a controlled flutter of long, real eyelashes. She had black hair short enough to reveal her ears, high cheek-bones and pointed features; she looked like an efficient elf—and a successful elf. George was able to afford Bineshaft Court's services because he successfully imported expensive EEC clothes, and he recognised Dr Gloria's Italian skirt, skirt and shoes. Even the white doctor's coat she wore had the initials of Yves St Laurent embroidered on its breast pocket. George was impressed and excited by her and even forgot his legs for a moment, which was precisely what he was supposed to do. Nothing at Bineshaft Court happens by chance.

The room George was shown into was cheerful and chintzy. Little flowers stippled the walls and curtains. Bigger flowers grew on the two small armchairs, which sat on a pale green lawn of carpet. The only indication that this was not a guest-room in a country house was the bed—the very latest in gleaming chrome, bristling with springs, hydraulic rams and digital read-outs. As he undressed, George could see the other patients out in the garden. They walked either with pain or with a sort of careful elation, depending on whether or not they had yet had Dr Ethics' miracle wrought on them. Suddenly George's legs hurt. He drew the curtains and got into bed.

There was a knock at the door. "Come in," said George, and the door opened and closed again. Maybe it was the half-light but no-one appeared to have come into the room. George fumbled for the light switch and found it.

"Down here," said a voice. Its owner, George saw, was standing by the side of the bed, and was fully three feet tall. "Sorry to surprise you. I'm DR TICH SERAGLIO. Come to give you your preliminary examination. Can you stand by the bed, please?"

George carefully eased himself on to the floor, and watched the top of the midget's head as he scuttled round George's legs. George felt occasional twinges as Dr Seraglio's measuring calipers moved gradually down, the width at each centimetre's descent being noted on what seemed an enormous clipboard with what seemed an enormous pen. The doctor chatted as he worked in a voice that sounded like a fourteen-year old boy's, occasionally swooping down into unfamiliar registers.

"Hope I didn't surprise you too much. I know it can be a bit of a shock. Some patients fall flat on the floor. That's the only chance I ever get to examine the top half of a body! Mostly it's legs. That's why I'm here, of course. It was more fun where I was before, in the harem. Forty girls' well-being under my watchful eyes, hee hee!" He gave a lewd chuckle. "The Sultan thought I'd be no threat, you see. Eastern men can be very unimaginative. And eastern women

32

very inventive! Hee hee! Exact height, please?"

"Six foot four," said George automatically.

"You haven't been sent by Celia, have you?" asked Dr Tich Seraglio.

"Celia?"

"DR CELIA SORIGHT. She runs the home for incurably tall in Chalfont St Giles. We get many of our patients from there."

"No," said George. "My doctor sent me. Er—is there a bedpan? I'm sorry, but. . ."

"Bedpan's no good to a chap your height," said the midget. "Here!" And he wheeled from the corner a pot mounted on top of a golf trolley. "There," he said, placing it in front of George's groin. "DR HIGO'S ARTICLE. Dr Higo's one of my colleagues and does a bit of inventing in his spare time. He came up with this the other day. Don't know where we'd be without it, having all you tall chaps about. No splashing and a pocket for your spare balls. Tee hee!"

George embarrassedly relieved himself, and a nurse arrived to wheel Dr Higo's article away.

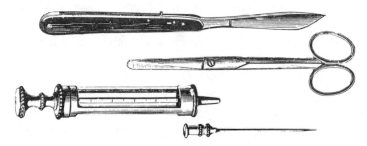

"On the scales, please," said Dr Seraglio. "Hmmm. A bit over, I'm afraid. You'll be on diet number three." He handed George a leaflet. "These menus are prepared for us by DR CALORIESIGHT and IGOR STARCH-DIET, our nutritionists. Diet number three is quite lenient. You get solid food on the fifth day. Now, back to bed, please. I shall take these measurements with me. We should have a pair of suitable legs within forty-eight hours. Then we'll whip yours off and stitch the new ones on. So for a couple of minutes in between, you'll be *my* height. Hee hee!" And with a wave of his enormous clipboard, the tiny doctor was gone.

★ ★ ★

In the basement, DOC IRA GERSHLIT put aside the half-bottle of vodka and read again the list of measurements. Another tall one. Where was he going to find another tall one? Not round here. Still, it was safer if he went further away. He stuffed the measurements in the inside pocket of his jacket and checked the contents of his bag. Hypodermic. Pain-killer spray. Saw. Picking up his car keys from beside the vodka bottle, he walked unsteadily out into the twilight.

★ ★ ★

Dr Gloria Ethics herself no longer practised surgery. She had had ambitions in her youth, until her introduction to medical accountancy had provided her with the vocation she lacked. She could now diagnose a patient's financial worth at a cursory examination. She could judge the side-effects of extras on a bill to a whisker. And she could cost her time and that of her staff to four places of decimals without drawing a breath. That was why she had hired DR IGOR H. ELASTIC to replace her in the operating theatre. He was productive. He was also a fairly reliable surgeon, and did as he was told. When a clamp was missing, he paid up. He did not read indemnity forms too closely. Dr Ethics was pleased with him, even though having two people called Igor on the staff made for confusion. (Still, no harm had been done on that one occasion. Indeed, the patient whose legs had been replaced by an unqualified nutritionist still sent an annual Christmas card with glowing thanks.)

George's torso moved up and down rhythmically on Dr Igor H. Elastic's operating table. Dr Elastic checked the legs he had removed from George against those which Doc Gershlit had obtained. A perfect match. Good old Ira! And no danger of sewing the old ones back on this time. The tattoos made that impossible; Dr Elastic hoped George wouldn't mind the tattoos.

Three days later George was still undecided about the tattoos. On one leg a fox ran desperately, its eyes wild and frightened. On the other a pack of hounds, two huntsmen and a dozen assorted riders galloped across a ploughed field. George looked at them again in the mirror in his room. Should the fox be chasing the hounds and the hunt? No matter. They didn't hurt, his new legs. He would happily live with inaccurate wildlife on his thighs if it meant no pain.

The next day he hid the unorthodox hunt inside his trousers, put on his shoes (the donor's feet were a different shape from his but, funnily enough, he found that wearing his own shoes on the wrong feet made them seem quite comfortable), paid his enormous bill and left. He felt well. Poor, but well. He felt so well that he had decided to walk to the station (which was fortunate as he had no money left for a taxi). Dr Gloria Ethics and her staff waved goodbye as he set off down the drive.

★ ★ ★

Doc Ira Gershlit cursed under his foetid breath as he started the car. Another six foot four in under a week! The last one had been tough. He'd had to go to Southampton. Six foot four wasn't easy to find. He turned left at the end of the drive, and saw the distant tall figure with the suitcase. "Oi," he whistled under his breath. "How lucky can you get? Six foot four. Exactly. Must be." He overtook the man, who gave a cheery wave. Ira Gershlit stopped the car and waited, his hypodermic already in his hand. He watched in the rear-view mirror as the figure approached the car, walking cheerfully but somehow untidily. Beneath the tall man's trousers, a wild-eyed fox dashed in hopeless pursuit of a baying pack of hounds.

Go Nurse!
(Surgeon)

'He gestured limply somewhere west of Ireland—"and this ridge of high pressure just keeps on coming toward us. I blame the sailors myself".'

CLOUDY
WITH GAY SPELLS

"TWO MINUTES ON FILM, studio, then to Osric for the weather."

The atmosphere in the television studio relaxed, for two minutes is a long time. In his corner by the weather charts OSRIC THIRDGALE was not relaxed. He felt sick. He wanted to go to the lavatory. Most of all, he wanted his mummy. It was Mummy who had made him apply for the job in the first place. Osric had been quite happy at the weather centre, drawing isobars and emptying the rain-gauge. Then the T.V. company had advertised for a new weatherman. Well, weatherperson in fact. It was this little semantic adjustment that caught Mrs Thirdgale's eye, she having few illusions about her son. "He may be a meteorologist," she said to her friend, Mrs Bestridge, whose Timmy was much the same, "but he still doesn't know whether!"

Osric's success in the job had been immediate. The flashing eyes, the mince from the Atlantic chart, the swooping giggle—all had transformed a worthy but boring item into the evening's most compulsive viewing. For thirty seconds the nation sat hypnotised by Osric's predictions for the following day's weather, with the combination of admiration and sympathy the British reserve for a circus liberty horse.

Osric didn't quite wear a plume on his head, but he was quite pleased with tonight's outfit. The T-shirt was cream, with an appliqué in chestnut glitter of a cloud, from which fell a spate of little cats and dogs. The brown calf trousers were fashionably baggy, but gathered at the ankle to show off the shoes—again cream, but with a gold lightning flash on each toe. Osric was pleased with the effect. Subtle. He hated anything gaudy.

To steady his nerves, he was counting his magnetic clouds—though tonight's forecast was good. He was on cloud nine when the floor manager started the countdown. The seconds ticked away. On zero, the red light on Osric's camera came on, the floor manager pointed an accusing finger at him and Osric, still wishing he had never accepted that third Dubonnet and eggflip in the club, pouted at the nation.

"Well," said Osric, "she said to me this morning did my mum, isn't it warm for October, she said, and I said, Mummy, I *have* to agree with you. Well I *do* have to, she gets furious if I don't and who wouldn't if you've brought somebody up and cleaned up their private little places and then all they do is argue with you. But she's right you know. It *is* warm. It's the warmest October since people started taking records and I wish people would stop taking my records. My friend Jeremy borrowed my 'Judy Garland live at Glenlivet' three weeks ago and it's as if it had never *existed*. The warmth, well it's over the Atlantic here"—he gestured limply somewhere west of Ireland—"and this ridge of high pressure just keeps on coming towards us. I blame the sailors myself. I mean if *I* arrived in port after weeks at sea *I'd* have a ridge of high pressure, know what I mean? Cheeky cats!"

He flounced over to the map of Britain. "And here's tomorrow's chart and its sun sun sun, all over again. I mean I'd love to stick a cloud on somewhere just to add a bit of je ne sais what to the board, but I can't, loves, it's just old Apollo beating down on all of us, which is nice if that's what you're into. Even here on the satellite piccy—well, you can see, can't you. Not a wisp. Not one. Just boring old England clear as clear, and if you imagine Scotland as a hat made out of fruit, d'you know the British Isles look a bit like Carmen Miranda sitting down. Must dash and I won't tell you who I'm seeing tonight but if *I* can sit down tomorrow I'll be *very* surprised. Sunshine all over tomorrow, why not go topless to the office, and the girls can please themselves. I'll leave you with the ridge of high pressure out at sea. Bye-bye, sailors."

With a wave calculated to quicken the heart of many a beardless deckhand, Osric was gone, and the nation sat back and ignored the following interview, in which the interviewer and author managed to mention the author's new book no less than seventeen times.

Osric collected his macramé bag and slipped out of the studio. As he did so, he bumped into the programme controller. "Sorry," said the controller, and did his captain-of-industry crinkle underneath his fine black eyebrows. "Just come down to see you. Wanted to say, bloody good. No really. Bloody good. Advertisers are delighted. Fifteen million. Regularly. D'you know something?"

"What?" said Osric. He wondered if the eyebrows were real.

"Your slot is now the most expensive in television," said the controller. He would have done his crinkle again, but he was unsure of the glue on one eyebrow. "Keep it up." He left.

"I should be so lucky," said Osric, and walked across reception to the swing doors.

"Goodnight, Osric," said the commissionaire, raising his good arm. "Fine tomorrow, then."

"Fine tomorrow and better tonight," said Osric, and walked out of the building. The usual early evening crowd was there, waiting for him. Ladies with shopping, three window dressers, four soldiers and a scout master, all holding out autograph books. Gaily Osric chatted and exchanged catty remarks as he signed their books. He was happy. Till tomorrow's nerves came on he was happy. As he stood, pen in hand, surrounded by admirers, he hardly noticed the snow begin to fall from the leaden grey sky above.

EVERAGE SPEED

The blokes at HI-GRIDE CASTROL speak in language
    fast and loose—
They have offices in Brisbane, and they're all of them
    called Bruce—
And they sponsor a drag racer at the track at Mount
    Saliva,
In the hopes that it'll help sell oil to every Okker
    driver.

Now one day Bruce Makarios (the man in charge of
    sales)
Just happened to be sticky-beaking down in New
    South Wales
When he came up alongside a Holden at a traffic
    light,
Which, when the lights went green, accelerated out
    of sight.

Bruce knew that he had just seen something nearing
    a sensation
(He'd never known a Holden with such acceleration).
And, since the sort of racing that he sponsored was
    called drag,
He knew that driver should be stowed in Hi-Gride's
    tucker-bag.

He caught him at the next lights and he waved him
    to pull in;
The other driver stopped, and grabbed the proffered
    Foster tin.

"My name is CRAIG HOTSLIDER,"he said. "This
    is my rod."
"I'm Bruce from Brisbane," answered Bruce. And
    Craig said, "You poor sod!"

Then Bruce explained that Hi-Gride would like to
    offer Craig,
A job to drive for them in—(he was sorry to be
    vague)
He couldn't say exactly how they'd use him at the
    start,
But certainly drag racing would constitute a part.

Craig hit Bruce firmly on the chin, Bruce fell as
    though for six,
Craig's Holden laid down upon the road two
    parallel tyre-slicks.
"Me, drag-racing?" he fumed, as the speedo went
    off the clock.
"You won't catch macho Craig Hotslider driving
    in a frock!"

When Bruce came round he rubbed his chin and
    got back in his car,
And drove straight back to Mount Saliva (which
    is pretty far),
Regretting Craig's recruitment hadn't been a great
    success,
So someone else would have to wear the Hi-Gride
    driver's dress.

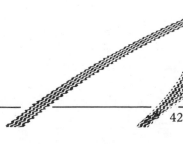

THE SPY WHO LOVED EVERYBODY

THE AIR WAS still crisp, even though it was nearly noon. Any day now, he thought, the thaw would begin. Then the drip, all day, as the snow left the pines. The icicles would lose their grip on the frozen gutters. It was not a time to sit near the house. He didn't like the thaw. The dripping could hide the sound of footsteps.

Unsteady rushes of falling snow produced noises that brought back too many memories. Though it was still quiet, he turned his chair to check behind him. The chair responded smoothly. It was a Bohringer 23L, the one with the big wheels at the front. He had had the narrower tyres fitted, and the department had added under the seat an electric motor from a green Harrods delivery van. The Bohringer could, for short bursts, sustain nearly seven miles an hour, with road-holding to match. Not that up here there was anywhere to run to. Vigilance: that was the only insurance up here. Vigilance. What was it that Hornby had said about the price of liberty? Hornby was right. Hornby was always right, damn him. He spun the chair round again and went on watching the cable which stretched down into the valley, listening for the hum that meant visitors. So far they had always been friendly visitors, but you could never be sure. Not now Hornby was dead.

The cable car was a Ferrugino SLC—not the new type with the nylon bearings which had caused the Bormiguera crash, but the old 8-person, 3875-kilogramme model, with the teak window sills. Many people consider it the finest cable car ever built, and second-hand ones change hands for prices that sound like oriental census figures. They were rare, Ferruginos, especially in this part of the world. But she was not surprised to see this one. She had known it would be here. She knew its serial number, and its date of manufacture. She knew it hung from a Machthoffer 72-strand cable, the type the Swiss used for the main bullion lift at the Geschweisserbank in Basle. She knew all about the cable, and the cable car. But about the man she was to meet at the top, she knew nothing.

The cable had been humming for some time now. Worse, the dripping had begun. He was worried. There had been no message. He opened the left arm of the wheelchair and checked the magazine. Empty. Damn the thaw. Quickly—more quickly than perhaps a younger agent would have done it—he wheeled himself into the chalet, across the Amtico tiled floor and into the kitchen. Between the Poggenphol units stood the refrigerator. It had no maker's name on it. "Strange," he thought. Opening the ice compartment, he took out a small rubber tray and peeled off its top half. Carefully he squeezed the eight bullets of ice into the spring-loaded clip in the arm of the chair. He filled the rubber bullet moulds with water and replaced the tray. Snapping the arm of the wheelchair shut, he went outside. He could see the cable car now, only three minutes away. Again he checked the arm of the chair. Sometimes one of the ice-bullets stuck. No, they were able to glide into place. The ice-bullets, too, had been Hornby's idea: as deadly as lead, but once inside the body they melted. No police force in the world could find a murder weapon with only a pool of water to go on. The device in the right arm of the chair, though, was his and his alone. A steel tube, eight inches long and half an inch thick, with a metal gauge on one end and a gun sight on top. Carefully he aimed it at the cable car and flicked a switch on the barrel. From the tube came the noise of the cable car amplified a hundred times. Systematically he moved the tube across the area where the cable car was. There it was. A heartbeat. He moved the device again. There were no other sounds. She was alone. He moved the detector until it picked up the heart again, stronger this time as the cable car approached. LUB-DUP, LUB-DUP, LUB-DUP. Definitely a woman. And standing up. But why, if she was alone in the cable car? The Ferrugino SCL had seats. Even the *later* Ferruginos had seats. So why was she standing up?

She had never regretted going to Rustington and Tearle for the crutches. They were balanced perfectly, thanks to the mercury filling, which even now expanded upwards as the crutches lengthened slightly in the mountain sun. They might be a little heavy, but there had been enough times when she had been grateful for that. Kaniusky would not attack her again in a hurry. She remembered the fight with Kaniusky, and her breathing quickened. Hundreds of feet above, the sensitive listening device registered the slight change in her heartbeat.

He heard the slight change, and waited. It was his turn for a paragraph, but he had nothing he wanted to put in it.

She looked around the cable car for something to describe.

★ ★ ★

He recognised her instantly when she stepped down from the

cable car. Now he saw why she had stood up during the long journey. Those legs, perfect to look at though they were, would not have lifted her out of the Ferrugino's deep Reccaro seats. She leant against the cable car's side, and he saw her press a button on the shaft of the crutches. Noiselessly the ends expanded to form two snow shoes. Like a swizzle stick, he thought. Easily she moved across the snow towards him, the light titanium net of the snow shoes preventing the crutches from plunging into the melting snow.

She did not recognise him until she was closer. Hornby had not told her who he was, only that she would recognise him. Recognise him she did, for she had studied his file many times when she was active. She knew him, and she knew he must know her, for in their time both of them had been the best.

When she was close enough for them to share a paragraph, he spoke.

"SHEILA TORRID, G.C., I presume." His voice was deep in the way only American voices can be, with still a hint of German in the throaty r's. "I assume you know who I am?"

"HORST GILDER, C.I.A.—and you can forget the G.C. They give us those instead of a decent pension. Mind if I sit down?"

"Make yourself at home. Just look out for falling icicles."

Leaning the crutches against the back of his wheelchair, she placed herself easily on his knee and kissed him on the mouth. The last vestiges of snow fell from the spokes of the chair's wheels.

"You mustn't," he gasped. "The doctor said one more and I've had it. Hornby should never have kept me active for so long."

"Hornby's dead," she said. "They've disbanded his section. All the hit men—everything."

"The entire Hornby Double-0 layout?"

"The whole thing. Controller, signals, stations, everything."

"Then it was all for nothing."

"Not quite. I'm here." She moved towards him again.

"Don't," he said. "Please don't. I'm sorry." He turned his head away, his face grey. It was getting cold again. She took out a rosewood George II matchbox and a pack of Elizabeth David herbal cigarettes. With perfectly steady hands she lit one, and threw the rosewood George II match away. She looked at him with pity. For fifteen years he had been attached to M.I.6. Very attached. Chief stud to the European section. In fifteen years he had, under Hornby's orders, seduced anyone and everyone who might have information the West could use. 653 times he had been activated. She had seen his file. No wonder he couldn't walk.

"I've seen your file," she said. "I understand."

"You don't know about the breakdown."

"653 women would make any man break down." She tried a light laugh. It didn't work.

"It wasn't 653 women. It was 604 women. And 45 men. God, those Russians are sods."

She looked puzzled. "That's only 649," she said. "What about the other four?"

"Sheep," he said. "We used them as couriers in Yugoslavia." He looked at her. "I still never got anywhere near your figure," he said, a note of admiration in his voice.

"You're near enough to it now." She rested her head on his

shoulder, and her finger tips slid like a pickpocket's between the buttons of his shirt.

He had read her file as well. Sheila Torrid. Born 1940 in Nailsworth, Gloucestershire. Expelled from Wycombe Abbey. Recruited—some said by Hornby himself—in 1956, and since then the finest sleeper in the whole of espionage. She had slept with 794 Warsaw Pact operatives in the field, and as many again in hotel bedrooms. No wonder she was on crutches. Damn Hornby. He kept everyone active too long. But Hornby was dead now. Hornby was dead. Then why could he hear Hornby's voice? For he could, quite clearly, in his right ear. The right ear against which Sheila Torrid was slowing moving her breast. Of course. She had a radio there. It was in the file. But why Hornby's voice? Hornby was dead. "Under the arms, Sheila," said Hornby's voice, "he likes being stroked under the arms." Hornby had sent her. Hornby was not dead. Hornby had sent her to kill him, in the only way she knew how, in the way the doctor had said would kill him.

He moved, as if in response, and she brought her head down to kiss him. He raised his face, and put his hands on her shoulders, pushing gently. She smiled, and took the hint. As she slid down his body, he waited for his moment. She would have to move sideways at one point, and her heart would be directly in front of the gun barrel in the chair's arm. The moment came, and he pressed the button. A thin trickle of tepid water oozed on to her camel hair coat, above the heart. There was a crackle as the dampness reached the radio with Hornby's voice on it. She looked up, hatred and pain in her eyes. He turned his head—there must be a weapon. He saw it, and reached out his hand.

"Don't touch my crutch!" she screamed furiously. But it was too late. His fingers reached it and, with a noise like a victorious football crowd, her crutch exploded. The birds rose from the dripping pines, and watched the ensuing avalanche cover the blood-stained terrace of the chalet.

★ ★ ★

In London, in an office high above St Pancras station, Hornby released the switch which had caused the explosion. He had been fond of Sheila and of Horst. But the Double-0 layout only stayed in being because it was ruthless. Hornby looked out of the window at the railway lines stretching into the distance. He could afford, after all, to lose a couple of sleepers.

Starring...

Narrow Bra is Bad
(Barbara Windsor)

Co-starring...

Mario P. Rocket
(Patrick Moore)

Guest appearance...

Henry L Hotly-Trumpet
(Humphrey Lyttleton)

FROM MY BOOKSHELF

LEA'S THIRD CORGI

NUMBER THREE in this popular series about a little Arab Princess and her dogs: *A Corgi for Lea, Another Corgi for Lea,* and now *Lea's Third Corgi.* The books are unusual within the canon of children's literature in that they were written by the computer in the marketing department of a well-known publishing house. In collating the results of a series of street interviews ("Do you buy books for your children?" "Why not?" "Well if you had any children would you buy books for them?"), the computer came to the conclusion that grown-ups buy children's books (and as it is grown-ups who buy children's books, so the books must appeal to the adult rather than the child, in much the same way that pet-food must appear appetising to the owner, not the pet. Very few pets actually buy

'The books were written by the computer in the marketing department of a well-known publishing house.'

their food—Arthur the cat, possibly, and the tea-drinking chimps, but not many others) for various reasons, but mainly two: royalty and dogs. The average grown-up reckons that a book without royalty or dogs is not worth gift-wrapping. So the computer set to, adding the Arab dimension so that the royal element could be incredibly rich, and also so that the Royal element could mistreat the dog. For it was felt that to appeal to children—who might then demand follow-up volumes of their own accord—the book should include the two things which children find most entertaining: physical torture and any mention of going to the lavatory. Thus Princess Lea treats her Corgi with merciless sadism, and he in return takes his revenge by fouling the more expensive rugs in the palace.

The success of the series is now publishing history, and the electronic author is now working (simultaneously) on *Lea and her Corgis, Yet Another Corgi for Lea, Six-Day Walkies*, and *Lea and her Corgis Go Shoplifting in Harrods.*

* * *

GHASTLIER DORIC
by GERALD I. OSTRICH

GERALD I. OSTRICH ("HISTORIC GERALD" as he is affectionately known in architectural circles) has for many years conducted his personal vendetta against classical architecture. He believes passionately in the supremacy of the Tudor era, and claims personal responsibility for the half-timbered revival in the 'thirties. He draws many parallels between our own age and that of Elizabeth I—it was, after all, in her time that inflation and round-the-world yachting were invented—and sees us now on the brink of tremendous prosperity. He is convinced that in between the two Elizabethan ages Britain became flaccid and hidebound, and blames this on the rise of rigid classicism in art, music and architecture. His figures on the change in the number of medals won by the army since the move from St James to Buckingham Palace (a decline he attributes solely to the change in the guardsmen's surroundings from Tudor to Classical) will be seen

*'For many years he conducted his
personal vendetta against
classical architecture.'*

as significant by some. Others will doubtles see the chapter headed
"Entasis—the architect's middle-age spread" as the nub of the
work. And all will be impressed by the beautiful illustrations,
particularly the publication of the plans of Blenheim, Chatsworth
and Castle Howard with detailed instructions for their
demolition. The book is handsomely produced, with a foreword
by the Minister of the Environment, and the fly-leaf bears the
quotation (from "The Old Orders" by E.K. Chesterfield) which
gives the book its name:
>"Speak to me not of your columns historic—
>Ghastly Ionian, ghastlier Doric."

Goat-herd Lirics

THE GOAT-HERDS of GRAITCLODSHIRE sing as they minister to their goats. Tourists who accidentally pass through that particularly unappealing county bring back tales of snatches of tuneless song heard in the few seconds before they could get the car windows up—a necessary manoeuvre since the Graitclodshire large horny roan (*capricornus priapus)* emits a smell which the urban nostril seldom finds attractive. The folk-songs of the goat-herds are, of course, principally an oral tradition. But one goat-herd once nearly learnt to write (though not to read—he tried, by taking a correspondence course in reading, but after six lessons had arrived and remained unread, the logical impracticability of this became apparent) and although unable to put the "tunes" down (and if you'd heard the "tunes", you too would enclose them in inverted commas, if not a sound-proof box) he was able to write down a phonetic version of the words which captures the jovial bawdiness of the original. They should be sung with red eyes, and while slightly dribbling.

"Tup Me"

Billy won't you tup me, tup me, tup me,
Billy won't you tup me, tup me in the grarse,
Billy won't you tup me, tup me, tup me,
Billy won't you tup me up the mountin pass.

"Standin' Up"

Billy said that standin' up
Was safe, I'm shure he did
Then why o why dere Nanny
Am I going to have a kid?

Goat-herd Lirics is reprinted from the only surviving copy. The goats ate the rest, along with the correspondence course.

CHARTED OIL RIGS

LLOYD'S OF LONDON, in their own interest, prepare this supplement to Admiralty charts, giving the positions of oil installations so far established around Britain. It is updated monthly, as new platforms either arrive or sink, and is made available to the shipping industry in the form of a cellophane grid which fits over the appropriate chart. In the first six months of its publication there was very little reduction in the number of direct hits scored by merchant ships on oil rigs—readers will remember the sinking of the 400,000-ton *Amoco Gipsy Moth* with the tragic loss of both of her crew. However, divers brought up the ship's papers and provided the clue that turned *Charted Oil Rigs* into a worthwhile publication. Though they had the oil rig supplement on board, they were unable to use it because they had no Admiralty chart to put it on. Since then, *Charted Oil Rigs* has been made available in a new size which fits the navigation literature carried by the average supertanker: the *Readers Digest It's-Fun-to-Learn School Atlas.*

I, Lord Reichstag

THE AUTOBIOGRAPHY of GISCARD O'HITLER, sometime president of Germany, Ireland and France, whose career is described elsewhere. First published in Paraguay.

* * *

IRIS THE GOLD CAR
by DORA E. GILCHRIST

FOR SOME YEARS NOW Ms Gilchrist has been writing her feminist children's books for the Harridan Press. Alice the Green Motorbike, Samantha the Blue Skateboard, Edna the Yellow Engine and Doreen the Red Bulldozer have all wheeled their confident way through the streets of Toyland despite the feeble efforts of the male population to put obstacles in their way. Now Iris the Gold Car joins the sisterhood, and if anything she's the

toughest so far. Committed children will love the way she subjugates her puny male driver, and roar at her escape from his efforts to re-spray her. As always, Iris emerges triumphant, and she captures the burglar Ethel despite the efforts of the plodding male policeman. With a foreword by Jill Tweedie.

★ ★ ★

IRGOT'S HERALDIC

IN 1951 RODERIC SLAIGHT was elevated from Gasmantle Pursuivant to be Irgot Herald, an achievement crowning many years at the College of Arms spent waiting patiently for people in the senior positions to die. His patience was rewarded, however—though in a way no one would have wished—when the previous Irgot Herald died in great pain after a thrombosis sustained during the 1951 Garter procession. Doctors agreed that the blockage was directly ascribable to his garter being too tight, and ironically it had been Roderic Slaight, his assistant, who had personally fitted the garter, since Irgot Herald was 83, which is old for bending down (though young for a herald). Imagine Roderic Slaight's grief, thinking that after so many years of waiting patiently, he might have been the unwitting cause of his master's early demise. However, with a notable display of selfless duty, he put sadness behind him and adopted the titles and office of Irgot Herald in ordinary. He then set about preparing his enormous and comprehensive book on the history and lore of heraldry. At its publication in 1975, the price of £128.99 was felt to put it out of the reach of most casual readers, but as undoubtedly the definitive work in the field it was bought by almost every library in the world. This resulted in a sale of over 10,000 for the first edition. Since then Roderic Slaight has produced an annual revision, also at £128.99, claiming to contain important and radical new heraldic developments. And out of sheer force of habit, libraries all over the world buy the new edition every year, thus providing Irgot Herald with a generous addition to the £33 per annum he gets paid by the College of Arms.

★ ★ ★

CARTIER, HIS GOLD

THE RECIPIENT of the coveted Maxwell House Coffee Table Book of the Year Award, this lavishly illustrated account of the legendary jeweller was the surprise best-seller of the Christmas season. You will love the story of the young Cartier, discovered with his father's gold watch and his mother's iron. When asked why he was ironing the innocent time-piece, he replied, "Making

it thinner, Papa!"

Prophetic words indeed. Much of the success of the book can be attributed to the unique launch it received. At the time of its writing the author, the publisher and Cartier's P.R. man buried a $200,000 Cartier necklace of marcasite and white gold somewhere in the western world. Clues as to its resting place are said to be concealed in the book. This caught the public imagination, and much speculation (and not a little digging) went on. So far, however, nobody has found the treasure. This state of affairs is likely to continue, since on the day after its original burial the author returned to the scene, dug up the necklace, sold it, and is now slowly but diligently drinking the proceeds.

★ ★ ★

RICH GIRLS DO EAT!

IONA KENWOOD, OLGA SILLY-DINNER and Paprika Cranberry-Venison tell you what to do with cream, brandy, truffles, peahen, platypus eggs, champagne and men called Alastair. Includes recipes for GRILED HARICOTS and HI-GLIDE CARROTS.

ISRAEL RIGHTCOD

HERMAN HAAR'S GREAT NOVEL of the North Sea. Young Israel Rightcod leaves his father's fish shop to take a job on board the trawler skippered by the obsessive Captain Mayhap, who sails the North Sea in constant search of the piece of cod which passeth all understanding. Icelandic gunboats, love outside territorial waters, and the final duel in which a great fish bites off Captain Mayhap's fingers, make this add up to the year's adventure novel most likely to be made into a disaster movie.

GHIRIDOR CASTLE
by ERIC D. GHOSTLAIR

ERIC D. GHOSTLAIR'S famous trilogy tells the story—no, more, recounts the saga—of Ferrodo, who with Palin, Walin, Malin, Hebrides and Rockall sets out in search of the wizard Notalf, Strom the Goblin and Ringo the Elf. After many adventures they arrive at the forbidding Castle of Ghiridor where a fearsome battle takes place, but finally Ferrodo, with his magic disc, puts a stop to it. All this takes three volumes of about 90,000 words each, and much of it is written in Peri, a fairy language invented by Ghostlair and comprehensible only to him.

Ferrodo made his first appearance in *Ferrodo Goes for a Troll*, a shorter children's book. When it became apparent that taller children were also reading it, the author expanded the story to its present scale. The cult-following that the books enjoy, particularly among students, has forced Ghostlair to leave his post as Geller Professor of Pananormal Studies at St Andrews and become a tax exile on the Isle of Man, where he divides his time between denying that his books are an allegory based on the Mitford family, and shouting at motor-cyclists.

LIGHTER "ORCADIS"
by DORIS LETHARGIC

The Poseidon Adventure, The Wreck of the Mary Deare, Hornblower R.N., Billy Budd, Sailing—A Joy for Life: many are the great books about the sea. Now, in the same tradition, comes *Lighter "Orcadis".* Seldom can Doris Lethargic's spare, nihilistic approach have found such fruitful ground as in this, the true life-story of a dumb coal-barge which spends sixty years moored, unused, in the river Humber before being broken up and scrapped. Winner of the 1982 Booker Prize.

COL. TIGER RASHID

I HADN'T SEEN Uncle Harry for years, so it was quite a surprise when his card arrived. No warning (there never is with Uncle Harry, my mother always says). "In town for a few days. Come and have dinner on Wednesday. Uncle Harry." That was all the card said. It was one of those plain white jobs with the sender's address across the top. It said "From the Endangered Species Club, Pickerings Court, St James's, SW."

I found the place pretty easily—Pickerings Court isn't very big, and "Endangered Species Club" was engraved on only the fourth brass plate I read. I gave my name to the porter, and asked for Uncle Harry. The porter scooted off to fetch him. I looked around the dimly lit hall. There was something about it that was different from other clubs I'd been to. I couldn't quite put my finger on it.

Uncle Harry came in. He had lost none of the impressiveness I remembered. Still the shock of hair shooting away from the forehead, the bushy moustache which jockeyed for position with the side-whiskers. And still the brilliant eyes, peeping out from lids which the sun had turned to walnuts, like two small animals hiding in a hollow tree. He wore an immaculate dark blue suit with a wide chalk-stripe, and plimsolls. He moved like a cat. (Well, he moved the way a cat would if it wore plimsolls). "Tony," he greeted me. "Good to see you. How's Mummy? How's Daddy? How's Nanny? Caroline? Pippa? Ned? Wonky?" I replied that they were all well. "Damned good," he said. "Come in and have a drink. Old enough now, aren't you?" I was in fact only seventeen, which he should have known, being my godfather as well as my uncle, but I didn't argue.

The bar of the Endangered Species Club was panelled, and again had that—well, *odd* feeling about it. "Sherry?" offered Uncle Harry. I nodded. "Felt I ought to say hello," said Uncle

Harry. "Godfather and all that. Haven't seen much of you. Thought we'd get to know each other. Thought you might like to see the club. Rum old place, isn't it?" I agreed that it was a rum old place. Uncle Harry went on, "Notice anything different? Look at the walls, old boy. Notice? No trophies. Not one."

So that was it! The walls, unlike most of the clubs Daddy had shown me, were completely free of antelope, bison, boar, lion or rhino. The floors as well had no skins on them. There was no sign of the normal elephant's foot waste-paper basket. And in the rexine armchairs, every one of the members sat reading their papers with their feet encased in pumps or slippers. Nowhere in the room was there any evidence that animals' lives were ever taken by man. In fact, the only ornament of any sort was a picture. I don't know what it was a picture of, for it was turned to face the wall so that only the back of the frame, the back of the canvas and the protruding ends of hardwood wedges were visible. Under the frame, on a small plaque on the wall, were the words "Col. 'Tiger' Rashid 1917-71."

'And in the rexine armchairs, every one of the members sat reading their papers with their feet encased in pumps or slippers.'

62

"The Endangered Species Club," said Uncle Harry, "was started by a few of us in 1964. Hunters, all of us. Killers, every one. We hunted, we fished, we shot. If it moved, we shot it. Then —well, I remember it almost exactly. Buffy Charlesworth rang me up one August and said he wasn't going with me to Kenya. Next morning, Dogs Anderson and Gerry Belwether rang up and said the same. And when Reggie Wincanton came on the blower I smelt a rat. I mean Reggie would no more miss a chance of taking a pot at a rhino than fly. So I knew something was up. D'you know what had happened?"

I shook my head. Uncle Harry looked thoughtful. "Ever heard of television?" he asked. I said I had. He looked surprised, and continued. "These chaps told me they'd seen this television thing, and were giving up killing things. They made me go round to Reggie's house—his man owned one of the receivers—and made me watch it. Only once. But once was enough." He looked thoughtful again.

"Lots of people say wildlife's one of the best reasons for having television," I said. "Was it a chap called Attenborough you saw?"

"No, not Attenborough," said Uncle Harry. "Met him since, of course. Nice feller. Kneels down a lot. No, no. Programme we all saw was called—er—Lenny the Lion. That was it. The next day we bought this place and started the club. Saving animals. That kind of thing."

"But Uncle Harry, why would Lenny the Lion make anyone give up big-game hunting?" I remembered Lenny the Lion from when I was a kid, and it seemed a bit—well, unlikely.

"Tony," said Uncle Harry seriously. "You're very young. Reggie and Dogs and Buffy and Gerry and I had knocked about a bit, but we'd never seen before a chap sticking his hand up a lion's jaxi and making its mouth move from inside. It just horrified us. It made us think about what we chaps did to animals. And so—well, we went the other way. Conservation. Bit nutty about it, you may think. Often the case, they say, with converts. Could well be true! But we do damned good work, though I say it myself. D'you know, since we started we've persuaded every single big-game hunter the five of us knew to give up. Well, nearly every one. All except one."

"Tiger Rashid?" I asked, and wished that I hadn't. For every head in the club turned towards me, took me in icily, and then remembered its manners and went back to its paper or its conversation. "Sorry, Uncle Harry," I said, "but it's written on the wall there."

"Well spotted, young Tony. But keep the voice down. Tell you what, we'll go in to dinner early. Then I can tell you the story without everyone earwigging."

* * *

I'm not a great one for vegetarian food normally, but I had to admit that the club chef did a jolly good job. Not that I had much time to concentrate on what I was eating, because Uncle Harry did tell me the most astonishing story during dinner. He started as soon as the *cotelettes aux noix* were served.

"I first met Rashid in Bhagalpur. He was in the army—our army. Odd how we met, actually. He—well, I suppose, not to beat about the bush, he saved my life. After a Polo accident. Damned thing went down the wrong way, and if he hadn't seen me choking and bashed me on the back with a punkah, I could have turned my toes up there and then. So we got chatting, the way you do when someone's saved your life, and he was one of those odd chaps—lot of them in India—who had sort of given up being Indian and gone overboard the other way. He talked as if he was in an Aldwych farce—you know, 'I say, spiffin' don't y'know, pip-pip, cheerioh, what-what-what?'—that sort of thing. Sounded odd, coming out of a brown face. Turned out he had been over here to school, gone to Sandhurst, and was now a Colonel in the Lancers.

"Well, I didn't see him for a bit, because our lot went up country to Katihar on a pig-stick, but when we came back to Bihar, there was a tiger-shoot. The local Nabob organised it. We all climbed on to the old jumbos, and the Nabob got into his Silver Ghost, and off we went to bag a few rugs. Now normally tiger-shoots were pretty over-rated. If you found a tiger at all it usually killed a couple of beaters and ran away before anyone could shoot it. But this time was different. There was a chap leading us, walking ahead of the first elephant, and he had the most uncanny knack of locating the tigers. Not only locating them, but sort of mesmerising them. They ambled up to him, gave him a friendly sort of look, and then walked down the line of elephants, as if he'd told them where to stand in order to get shot. We got seventeen in the one afternoon. I got one myself. You've got it at home, haven't you?"

I told him we had. It used to lie on the floor in the morning room, but had been banished to an attic since my kid brother jumped out of the linen cupboard wearing it and gave Nanny a stroke.

Uncle Harry went on. "Well, at one point towards the end of the day, this chap at the front turned round and I caught a glimpse of him. And d'you know who it was?"

"Col. Tiger Rashid?" I ventured. Uncle Harry looked at me, surprised.

"Have I told you this story before? No matter. Col. Tiger Rashid it was, the very same that had helped me spit out peppermints in Bhagalpur. They called him 'Tiger', I gathered from the Nabob, because—well, obviously because he had this knack with the big cats, but it went deeper than that. Evidently when he was a baby he actually lived with a litter of tiger cubs and was brought up with them, like that boy with the wolves. No-one knew how he got there, but you get a lot of abandoned babies around Bhagalpur. Energetic chap, the Nabob. No-one was untouchable to him! Anyway, one day the female got herself shot, and the beaters found this Rashid fellow toddling about with the orphaned cubs. They brought him in, and the Nabob brought him up as if he was his own which, as I say, was a pretty fair assumption. Sent him to school in England. Eton. Then to Sandhurst—well, I told you all that. He'd told me himself when I met him. And of course I met him again that day, after the shoot. I wondered whether I could broach the subject of his, to say the least, unorthodox upbringing. I needn't have bothered. He came right out with it. 'Harry, old fruit!' he cried. 'Ripping to see you again. Have the chaps given you the lowdown on my stripy kith and kin? All true, old bean. Many have been eaten by tigers, but I'm the only Tiger who's ever been to Eton, what?' and he laughed, sort of cackling—the way your Indian does.

"I was going to ask him more, but again he butted in. 'Now, Harry, I can see you're dying to know why I get involved in tiger-shoots and don't I find it a morsel beyond the pale? Every Tom, Dick and Harry asks me that, and you're a Harry so I knew you would, what?' He cackled again, and went on. 'Bullying, Harry. Beastly thing. All I remember about the tigers. I remember them bullying me in a beastly, rotten way. So I get my own back. I went to see a trick cyclist about it, don't y'know, and he explained it to me.' Well, that was interesting, but what I wanted to know was how he did it—how he found the tigers and dominated them, as I'd seen him do that afternoon. But when I asked him about that he sort of glanced it through the slips, as it were, and went on about knowing a lot of other chaps who'd been bullied and would be only too happy to see their big brothers and sisters on the wrong end of a big-game rifle. His eyes went funny while he said it. I don't know whether it was being brought up by tigers, or just going to Eton, but something had certainly made him determined to take his revenge.

"Anyway—cut a long story short, eh?—we didn't see each other for a few years, and then the club got started and I thought I'd write to him and ask him to join. I got the most venomous letter back, full of words like traitor and turncoat and toad-eater and such; really quite rude. So I didn't pursue it, but got on with forming the club with the others."

I looked round at the others. We were back now in the club's bar. All but two of the other members had gone. One was reading a back number of *Vole,* and the other, as he had been since I first came into the club, was fast asleep in the darkest corner with a newspaper over his face.

Uncle Harry went on. "One of our first campaigns, funnily enough, was the tiger. At one time they were down to a hundred in Bengal, where the best ones are. We got them protected. The Nabobs were very good about it on the whole, but I got a letter from the one I told you about whose shoot I'd been on years ago. He said that Rashid, on hearing that the Bengal tiger was nearly extinct, had seen it as a personal challenge, and had set off

immediately with a rifle and a hundred bullets, his eyes funnier than ever. Well, I told the other chaps about this, and we had a council of war, as it were, and decided there was only one thing to do. If the tigers weren't to become extinct, then Col. Rashid must.

"Six of us set off—myself and five others who'd known him at

Eton. We went up country from Cooch Behar. The locals said he'd passed through there a few days earlier. And we tracked him through the forest. All of us, remember, were hunters. We could read a spoor as easily as the *Sporting Life*. Not that he was difficult to track, for there were traces of him everywhere: half-smoked Passing Clouds, miniatures of port, copies of the *Tatler*. It was almost as if he wanted us to find him. And find him we did. At first light, in a clearing just north of Tikkapore, there he was, drinking tea and fretting over the house prices in *Country Life*. He turned when he saw us and raised himself on his hind legs, his eyes yellow and staring, his teeth bared in a fearsome snarl. We all fired at once, as we'd agreed we would." Uncle Harry went silent, and I leant forward.

"What happened, Uncle?"

"Oh, I'm afraid the head was ruined. We must all have hit him. But the skin was perfect. Absolutely perfect."

"The skin, Uncle? Tiger Rashid's skin?"

"Does sound a bit odd to you, young Tony, I suppose. But we were hunters. We were killing something that preyed on other animals. And a hunter's proof of success is the trophy. So we brought him back."

"Back here?" I looked around, half expecting to see Colonel Rashid spread face down on the floor.

"Of course. As a warning to all of us. As a reminder of our position as part of the animal world. Mind you, not everyone would understand, so we couldn't have him as a rug. And we have ladies' nights now sometimes. So we had to put him somewhere he wouldn't attract attention. Somewhere he could fade into the background. Camouflage, y'know—second nature to a hunter. So we. . .well, see for yourself. See if you can spot our only trophy."

I followed his eyes as they travelled round the room. Apart from us, there was now only one other occupant. Sitting motionless in the darkest corner, with a newspaper concealing the damage the Endangered Species Club had wrought, were the remains of Col. Tiger Rashid.

"You've got him, Tony," said Uncle Harry. "He always was a bit of a stuffed shirt."

I SEE NO SPONSORSHIP

"THERE HE IS. Port side, ten o'clock, about 400 yards." The voice crackled in his headphones, and the pilot eased the big R.A.F. Nimrod round to port. Dead ahead was what they'd been looking for—the red, white and blue triangle that was propelling ROGER DITCHSAIL's sailboard across the Atlantic. As they passed overhead, he waved. He was all right.

"All right" is a relative sort of a term. Roger Ditchsail didn't *feel* all right. For nine days now he'd been standing on the sailboard, nine days of fighting with the patriotic nylon triangle that tried to pull him into the water. Twice it had succeeded, and he had gone in. Twice he had hauled himself back on to the fibreglass leaf that was to take him to America. The second time, he made the decision. He'd pay back the sponsorship money. *Observer* or no *Observer*, using the typewriter was just not on.

BRITISH INDUSTRY
-OR-
"A THOUSAND GILDERS?
COME - TAKE FIFTY!"

I SING OF the beginnings of a famous movement
That some people think has been a great
      improvement.
Others disagree and think it a bad thing,
For 'tis of the trades unions that here I sing.
Some of you reading this may well be astounded
To find out just how long ago they were founded.

Come back with me now, if you will, to the day
When in what we now call Avon there held sway
A ruler strict and terrible and frigid
Who went by the name of CARLOS THE RIGID.
(Actually we don't know if he was frigid or not
But words like "rigid" put the poet in a spot.)

Anyway, this Carlos the Rigid fellow
Had a chariot he wanted painted yellow,
But his wife, Florence, said, "Come, be bold,
Eric up the road had his one in gold."
"Yes, dear," said Carlos, who went through life
Frightened of nothing but his lady wife.

Down the hill went Carlos in his chariot
(At one point, o'er a stream he had to carry it)
Till he came at last to his own village,
Which he had captured with the sword and pillage
And a bit of rape. There, next door to the builders,
He saw a sign saying "Acme CHARIOT-GILDERS.

By appointment to the Duke of Berwick,
And the Earl of Andover, and Eric."
Carlos thought, "This must be the right shop,"
And put his foot over the doorstop,
Went inside, where stood in rough attire,
A man who turned and uttered, "Morning, squire.

My name's Garric, gilder of this city,
That your chariot outside? My, but she's pretty.
Want it gilded, do you, want it customised?
Quite right, squire, it's time folk realised
That chariot-gilding's now become a must—
Besides it helps protect the frame from rust."

Carlos the Rigid left the chariot at his gate
With promises of a firm written estimate
And thought no more about it for some days,
Though found that on his pillaging forays
The spare chariot he borrowed from his wife
Had on each wheel a much less effective knife.

But he managed. And upon the seventh day
He found when he came home (he'd been away)
A letter from the chariot-gilding concern
Which really gave him quite an unpleasant turn:
For the employment of his gilding arts
Garric had quoted thirty-three pounds, not including
      parts.

Carlos was horrified and went off in haste,
Back to the village where the gilding shop was
      placed,
Where stood old Garric, who had sent the quote.
Carlos said, "I ought to chuck you in the moat.
Give me my chariot back, or you'll be severely
      killed."
"Piss off," said Garric. "We have formed a guild.

'For the employment of his
gilding arts,
Garric had quoted thirty-three
pounds, not including parts.'

All of us gilders have got together
Because what with gold going up, and the cost of
    leather
And other things necessary for making chariots
    handsome,
It is necessary for us to charge a king's ransom.
So in future if you want anything gilded from a
    chariot to a trumpet,
You can pay our prices, matey, or frankly, lump it."

Carlos the Rigid faced the gilder stolid
And said, "I dub you now GARRIC THE SOLID.
You know that chariot-owners have no choice
If those who gild speak with a single voice.
We'll have to pay your price or face our wives,
To do which would be more than the worth of our lives."

But Florence, and the other squires' spouses,
All said, "Take no notice of those common louses—
To tradesmen we will never be beholden.
Eric's chariot looks common with all that gold on."
(You will of course remember Eric up the road,
Whose gilded chariot positively glowed.)

From that day on Carlos the Rigid didn't stop
Whenever he passed Garric the Solid's shop,
And nor did anyone else—they all passed by.
The chariot-gilder's art began to die:
The chariot-gilders may have owned the gold
But benefitted not, for none was sold.

Likewise the chariot-owners suffered too,
For when the winter's cold turned noses blue,
On all the roads around the village it snowed
And, unprotected by gold, then did corrode
The axles of each chariot, you see,
Until not one would have passed its M.O.T.

One by one, as a result of all the atmospherics
The chariots fell to pieces, except for Eric's.
But one day from outside his house, Eric's was
      nicked
(They never found by whom but it was probably a
      Pict).
So now the world of chariots is bereft.
You look around—there's not a solitary one left.

And all because the chariot-gilders united,
Put up their prices and their business blighted.
Though the customers, too, must take some of the
      blame
For, in times of rising prices, expecting to pay the
      same.
Any road up, it made chariots disappear,
And gold is still, not to put too fine a point on it,
      pretty dear.

History

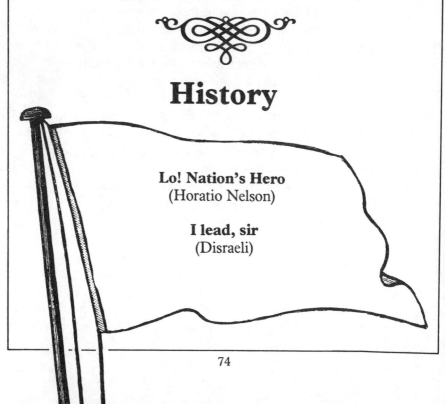

Lo! Nation's Hero
(Horatio Nelson)

I lead, sir
(Disraeli)

THE CRICKET MATCH

EVER SINCE a life assurance company began to sponsor Test matches, the City of London has taken a renewed interest in cricket. Of course, the City has had for years the oddity of its own cricket field. It lies between the City Road and Bunhill Row, and since 1538 the Honourable Artillery Company have played cricket on it, despite the fact that if they stopped playing cricket on it and sold it to a developer, they could probably buy another twenty million pounds worth of artillery.

You might think it surprising that a group of part-time soldiers enjoy such expansive and expensive sporting facilities, in view of the fact that the City's other major cricket club has no home ground at all. But the City's other club is of recent formation. The H.A.C. annexed its oval before property prices passed through the false ceiling, the insulation and the roof in the 'sixties. The P.C.C.C. had no chance to show such foresight, as this is their first season. They are the Post-Cardiac City Cricket Club. To join, you have to be a City businessman who has survived both a major heart-attack and the ministrations of a particular heart specialist whose sworn opinion it is that heart sufferers should thenceforward play cricket, since it gives gentle exercise and cannot possible excite. This, anyway, is his theory. At first, all went well. The P.C.C.C. turned up gently and punctually at eleven villages on eleven Saturdays, and each time managed to engineer the result most dear to the true cricket-lover's heart—a draw interrupted by rain.

In truth, the itinerant nature of the team is their own choice, spurred on by their doctor. He feels that these trips to havens of rural peace are as therapeutic as the game, serving to remove his ex-patients from the City with its associations of competition and stress. Had he decided otherwise—that the team must grasp the nettle and play always within the City, to exorcise their ghost by meeting it first bounce and despatching it over long-on—then the

H.A.C.'s ground might have been under threat. For the P.C.C.C.C.'s dozen or so founder-members were among the richest men in the City, in England, in Europe, probably in the World, and raising twenty million pounds between them would have been the work of the few moments it takes to oversubscribe a new share issue. But their specialist had doomed them to wander the village greens of England and so they did as they were bid, for they believed it made them able to carry on juggling seven different burning currencies with two hands from Monday to Friday in the City, not half a mile from the H.A.C. ground.

★ ★ ★

The twelfth Saturday of their existence found the P.C.C.C.C. at TOILCHARD REGIS in Wiltshire, not far from Marlborough and not far from Hungerford, but not very near to either. Too far from London to commute, but too near to escape its influence. Much of Toilchard Regis is thatched unnaturally well, as second-home buyers have moved in and improved the houses to the point where no native of Toilchard Regis can afford them any more. Luckily, a large group of speculative post-war houses was built to attract people to the village. These now house the locals, who got them quite cheaply, the newcomers having eyes only for the thatch, the beams, the bread oven and the inglenook. Toilchard Regis's cricket team divides roughly half and half—well, exactly, not roughly, since most Saturdays either ten or twelve turn up and insist on playing—between seven-day-a-week residents and two-day-a-week residents. Of a Saturday they meet before lunch at the Bull and Bear on the village green, where they have a clear view of the cricket pitch and usually the opposition—for visiting cricket teams also tend to sniff out the nearest pub to soothe the effects of the journey, to try and catch a glimpse of the home side, to ask the landlord what they might expect in the way of fast bowling, reliable batting or (worst of all) a proper wicket-keeper, and generally to analyse the atmosphere of the alien planet on whose surface they find themselves.

Thus it was that Joe Painter, Alan Tremoyne, Ned Deering, Tom Deering, Jim Trance and the others sat and watched while

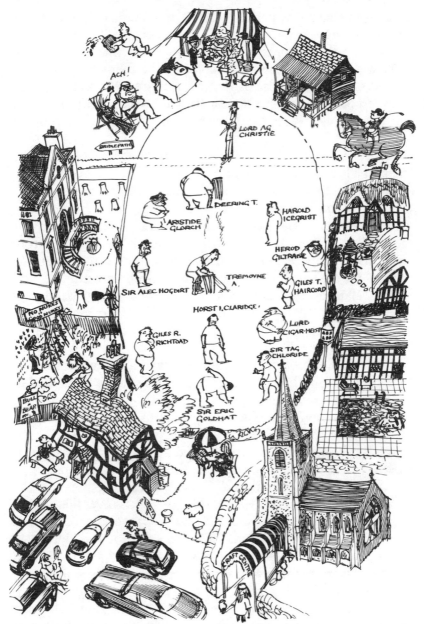

The Toilchard Regis Cricket Ground at 5.07 pm on Saturday, 20th June 1981. Lord A.G. Christie's field-setting before bowling the final ball.

the Bull and Bear's car park filled with two Daimler Double-Sixes, two Range Rovers, a Maserati Bora, a Porsche Turbo, a black Renault 5 with a telephone in it and four Silver Shadows (three of them with race-horse mascots replacing the flying lady). These, instead of the more normal motor-coach, represented the team transport of the eleven heart patients who now stood in the saloon bar, holding eleven neat tonic waters in eleven slightly shaking hands.

The rules of village cricket decree that, at about 1.30, the two teams shall set off from the pub to the pavilion, and on the way shall pretend to have seen each other for the first time. So it was that at 1.32, halfway across the village green, Alan Tremoyne of Toilchard Regis turned to the man who had walked with him for the last hundred yards or so and said, "You'll be the chaps from London, I suppose. My name's Tremoyne. I'm the village captain, for my sins." He smiled, and stuck out a hand.

His walking companion took it in a larger, redder hand, and shook it briefly. "Hogdirt," he said, "Alec Hogdirt. Well, SIR ALEC HOGDIRT, if you insist. Not ashamed of it. It was these hands got it for me."

"Are you the captain, er, Sir Alec?" asked Tremoyne.

"I am not, son, though there are those as says I should be. Oh yes. Alec, they say, you should be captain. Well, *Sir* Alec, in fact, they say, but I don't stand on ceremony. But I'm not captain, and that's that, so I pull my weight and bide my time, Sir Alec or no. You want the General, Sir Eric." And he indicated a tall, brown husk of a man with a grey toothbrush tethered to his upper lip.

"Are you all Sir Something?" Tremoyne asked.

"Nay lad," said Sir Alec. "Just three of us. Eric over there, Tag, of course, and me. Sir Alec. I got mine eight years ago. Tag's is only two years old. Eric got his for being in the army. It didn't cost him a penny, so it doesn't really count. But they still made him captain. There are those who say that this country's decline is due to that kind of thinking, and I'm not saying I'm not one of them. But that's how it is. General!" he shouted, and the long, pale linen jacket ahead stiffened, and turned slowly. "This is the home team's captain. He thought I was the captain. Easy mistake to make. I told him you were captain. For the moment." Sir Alec looked belligerently at the general, who stared past him at Tremoyne, and offered a dessicated hand.

"SIR ERIC GOLDHAT is my name," he said, pleasantly enough. Alan Tremoyne took the hand. "Tremoyne," he said. "Alan Tremoyne."

The General looked interested. "Tremoyne, eh? Any relation of D.R.T. Tremoyne? Green Jackets?"

"Not that I know of," said Alan. "Sorry."

"B.J.M.?" said the General.

"I beg your pardon?"

"B.J.M.," repeated the General. "B.J.M. Tremoyne. Younger brother of D.R.T. Got a D.S.O. in Burma."

"I don't think any of my family was in the army, sir," Alan explained.

The General looked at him suspiciously. "You're not Welsh, are you?" he asked after a pause.

Alan pretended not to hear and changed the subject. "Don't you think we ought to toss, sir?" he said. The two teams were now moving into the pavilion in dribs and drabs, and it was getting late.

The General agreed, and asked his players if any of them had any money. They all denied possession of the smallest sou, as they did regularly to all inquiries. No really rich man ever admits to having any money. "Liquidity problem," said Sir Eric. "What would you do if you won the toss?"

Alan hesitated. "Put you into bat, sir," he said.

"Set yourself a target, eh!" barked Sir Eric. "Good ploy. I always bat first meself. Not saying you're not right. No need to toss, though. We bat first. Good decision, young Tremoyne. Tell me, were your father's initials S.E.J.?"

"No sir, T.K.A." replied Alan.

"T.K.A., eh?" mused the General.

"No, just one 'A'," said Alan.

The General looked at him, and again wondered if he was Welsh.

★ ★ ★

It was only five minutes past two when, to the surprise of the Toilchard Regis faithful, the umpires came out. By the standards of village cricket, this is punctuality almost to the point of pedantry. But the P.C.C.C.C., for all their lack of a coin to toss up with, were not men who had earned their millions by turning up late. Each one, invalid or no, was in his office every morning before his secretary, to sort through the mail and see which letters were for her to pass to him, and which for her to pass on to the groundlings. So the P.C.C.C.C. batting order was already on a typed slip of paper. The presence of a scorer and two umpires had been checked by phone and confirmed by letter (by one of the secretaries who arrived at the office after the team members). Indeed, the delay of five minutes was only due to the absence of a wicket-keeper's glove, which had been borrowed by the wife of the wicket-keeper to remove the vol-au-vents from the oven, so they would have plenty of time to go cold before the tea interval. The glove having been returned, Alan Tremoyne (an efficient, if rather harrassed, person and a trainee estate manager) led his ten men on to the field, full of hope that the eleventh would arrive when he saw the rigours of fielding waning, and the chance of a bowl and a bat waxing.

The opening pair of millionaires were Sir Alec Hogdirt (whom we have met, who had progressed from Pigs to Bacon to Pork Pies to Wholesale and Retail until he controlled all food that grunted from squealing piglet to smoky-bacon-flavoured crisps and pork scratchings) and GILES T. HAIRCORD, whose capacity for seeing carpet in terms of acres rather than square yards had made him at thirty-four very rich and very worried. His carpets had made him a pile, his friends said. He had piles, his enemies said. Either way, his incipient angina had greatly strengthened the team's batting, as had the fact that, though ambitious and greedy, he was hardly mad at all. As the Toilchard Regis clock struck eight, he looked at his digital watch. It was 2.06.00 (and 10.06.00 in Perth, Western Australia. It was that sort of watch). Sir Alec took middle and leg from the local magistrate, looked round the field and began to pat Wiltshire with his bat.

In village cricket, each bowler's first ball is special. The batsman has no idea whether the new bowler is fast, medium slow, an absolute rabbit, keen but mediocre, a man with a grudge against batsmen, or worst of all, a halfway competent cricketer. The batsman finds out all these things during the first few seconds. This makes that first ball harder than anything Test cricket has to offer. In Test cricket the bowler is Lever, left-arm fast-medium, tending to swing the ball in. In village cricket the bowler is the grocer, and the umpire thinks he's right-handed from the way he works the bacon slicer.

So with trepidation Sir Alec Hogdirt faced the first ball from the Toilchard Regis grocer, Joe Painter. It turned out to be a fast in-swinger, but only the square-leg umpire could see whether or not it swung before it whistled past him. The magistrate signalled four wides. Two German tourists in deck chairs consulted each other on what this might mean. Giles T. Haircord walked over to the point where the ball had bounced—a point about fifteen yards away from the pitch—and prodded it. He was wondering whether to open more branches of Ambience, a chain of shops he had successfully started which sold uncomfortable knotty-pine beds and corduroy curtains, or merely to take over Environ, his principal rival. He was still wondering when the grocer bowled his second ball, a mirror image of the first, which hit cover point in the kidneys on its way to the boundary. "Next one should be bang on middle stump," said the umpire cheerfully, lowering his arms once the scorer had acknowledged four more wides. It was, and it duly bowled Sir Alec Hogdirt, who stood his ground firmly until the umpire raised his finger, then glared at him and walked sullenly towards the pavilion, crossing as he did so the incoming batsman, who was the frozen-food magnate, HAROLD ICEGRIST.

A small, dogged man with a healthy doormat of grey hair, Harold Icegrist came from Barnsley and therefore believed himself invincible at all forms of sport. This belief generally stood him in good stead, since self-confidence daunts an opponent more than almost anything else. He and Giles T. Haircord took the score to 31 before Giles T. Haircord was run out. Well, hardly run out, because he made no effort to run at all, standing instead deep in concentration. (It had just occurred to him that to bring the

South Korean occasional tables in through Ireland might avoid the tariff controls—if not even attracting a subsidy.) He smiled sheepishly, collected his pocket calculator from the umpire and departed. The two German tourists clapped politely, and checked their rule book.

Harold Icegrist lasted not much longer, giving his wicket away in order to be back in the pavilion for a three o'clock transatlantic phone call. By the time he had hung up the P.C.C.C.C. had scored 65 for 4 with LORD. A.G. CHRISTIE not out 11 and Sir Eric Goldhat not out 9, the innings of ARISTIDE GLORCH, the shipping magnate, having lasted only two balls. It should be said that the first of these went for six over square-leg. The second went to the same place, but this time square-leg did not get out of the way in time and was forced to catch the ball to save himself serious injury.

It is a fine thing to watch two old English patricians at the wicket. Arthur Gervaise Christie, six foot three of him from his grey socks to his bald head, like a Georgian folly topped by a dome, and Sir Eric Goldhat, nearly as tall but with an Old Wellingtonian tie holding up his trousers in contrast to Lord A. G. Christie's Etonian one. As they cantered their sweetly stroked runs, they looked like a pair of threadbare greyhounds with striped girths. Lord Christie's fifty was followed by Sir Eric's, and their success so demoralised the Toilchard Regis team that the batsmen who followed them were also able to score freely—apart, that is, from the merchant banker HEROD GILTRAISE, whose company, GIRO CASHIER LTD, had doubled its value in the previous week thanks to judicious investment in the Middle East. Thinking of the Middle East, Herod Giltraise remembered that he should not be playing cricket on a Saturday and his concentration suffered.

When the post-cardiac team's innings ended at 4.28, the score sheet read like this:

Sir Alec Hogdirt b. Painter	0
Giles T. Haircord run out	14
Harold Icegrist c. Trance b. Tremoyne	16
Lord A.G. Christie not out	77
Aristide Glorch c. Deering N. b. Deering T.	6
Sir Eric Goldhat lbw b. Painter	51
Horst I. Claridge c. Trance b. Deering T.	22
Sir Tag Chloride hit wkt b. Jordan	24
Giles R. Richtoad c. Tremoyne b. Deering T.	18
Herod Giltraise b. Jordan	0
Lord Cigar-Heist ret hurt	1
Extras (w. 8, nb. 1, leg byes 2)	11
Total	240

So it was in cheerful mood that the team sat down to tea (well, LORD CIGAR-HEIST didn't sit down, the wild stumping attempt from Jim Trance having hit him firmly on the coccyx), for 240 is a formidable score in village cricket. They might even win! The Post-Cardiac City Cricket Club had never yet won a match. Normally they batted for a gentle couple of hours, scored ninety or so, had a frugal tea, misfielded for an hour while the home team approached their score, got rained on, shook hands with everyone and drove home. But today—well, it was obviously the arrival in the team of Lord Christie (promoted on the death of SIR GODRIC LEATH, the Governor of the Bank of England, who had been run over while trying to pick up a penny that had rolled into the middle of the North Circular Road) which had strengthened the side. None of them knew him well. He was not a City man generally, but he came up from the country occasionally to try and attract sponsorship for the ballet festival he ran at his house, Glen Underboy, and several of them had been approached in this capacity. Well, none of them was averse to sponsoring art if the

return was reasonable, and if he went on playing his late cut as sweetly, Lord Christie could look forward to an easier passage in the future. "Perhaps he might be able to bowl as well," they said to one another. And with this pleasing thought in mind, they sat down to tea.

The wives of the Toilchard Regis team had excelled themselves. They had not only cooled the vol-au-vents, but had curled the sandwiches and dried the tops with a hair-dryer. The biscuits had been dampened, the fairy cakes' chocolate icing had been melted, then allowed to set again. Scones of a weight to rival uranium—and roughly as beneficial to the human body—had been buttered with butter whose sell-by date had long passed. There were flapjacks of a consistency to challenge the whole false-teeth fixative industry and sticky things made of weetabix and cocoa, while the sandwich fillings—the work of Mrs Deering (N)—were a tour de force: white of egg with cress and earth, cheese and mould, hundreds and thousands with lemon curd, and ham fat; each one a noble complement for the furry aluminium pot of already sugared tea. With 240 on the board, the P.C.C.C. tucked in—so much that when the four strongest ladies carried in the fruit cake, the magnates could manage scarcely two slices each. The remainder had to be sold to the two German tourists, who gave every sign of approval at being charged only 94p a slice, for they too had been to London.

When the teams returned to the field, it turned out that Lord Christie could indeed bowl. Sir Eric Goldhat invited him to take the second over instead of Sir Alec Hogdirt, who had expended so much energy in telling everyone how he had been unfairly dismissed that he was now too tired to bowl. The first over had been bowled by SIR TAG CHLORIDE, founder and managing director of DIGITAL SCHROER, a multinational whose purpose was clear to very few people below presidential rank. Sir Tag had conceded four wides and two runs, from a lucky snick by Ichabod Jordan over the head of the P.C.C.C.'s other Giles, GILES R. RICHTOAD, who was to assets what Nitromors is to paint. His concentration at what the rest of the team called 'first strip' was impaired by his listening throughout the game to a long memo from a New York colleague on his miniature earphone.

Lord A. G. Christie's first over was bowled at a speed which would not have disgraced Larwood himself (on whose style it was based). The effect was the more terrifying for the loud grunt that accompanied the delivery of the ball, and for the fact that Lord Christie did not stop when the ball left his hand, but carried on running down the wicket as if helpless without a braking parachute. This so surprised the opening batsman that he watched the progress of the galloping peer rather than the ball, which whistled unheeded past him and dislodged his off stump. His successor was less distracted, and played carefully forward—only to find himself caught by the bowler who had got within five feet of overhauling the ball. At the end of two overs the Toilchard Regis team were 6 for 2 and even some of the wives had come out of the pavilion to watch. They stood, ranged directly behind the bowler's arm, drying plates with flapping white tea-cloths.

The city cricketers clapped Lord Christie warmly on the back, and took their places for Sir Tag Chloride's next over. A new spirit was abroad. Better, a new spirit was in Wiltshire, which isn't abroad at all. Sir Tag's over conceded but one run, and that should have been a boundary but for Aristide Glorch throwing himself—nay, hurling himself—into the path of the ball, and returning it to the wicket-keeper with a smile his face had not seen since the invention of flags of convenience.

That same wicket-keeper's moment of glory was yet to come. After six overs, with the score at 29 for 6, Sir Eric Goldhat felt emboldened to change the bowling and allow his off-breaks their weekly outing. As he ran up he saw to his surprise that the wicket-keeper was standing right behind the stumps, not twenty yards back as he usually did. HORST I. CLARIDGE, hotelier and restaurateur, was remembering the happy days at G. CARRIDI'S HOTEL, when he was reception clerk. And now, again, he had moved from the office at the back to the front door. Let no cricket ball try to pass *him* without a tie! Sir Eric duly bowled, the demoralised batsman duly played and missed and Horst I. Claridge, sweating a little, gathered the ball and removed the bails as if spinning a visitor's book round to face a guest. "Porter!" he cried, forgetting himself for a moment. And the umpire, who was very deaf, raised his finger. Sir Eric Goldhat ran to congratulate the keeper, his Adam's apple bobbing furiously.

From then on, as each wicket fell, the Post-Cardiac Cricket Club ran excitedly to whoever was responsible and patted him, talking volubly, congratulating each other and giving little jumps. They were going to win. They liked winning. They were used to winning from Mondays to Fridays, but not used to winning at cricket. They were going to win, and it wasn't even going to rain.

When Alan Tremoyne came out to bat, his side had 43 runs on the board for the loss of nine wickets. The faces of the fielders were almost derisive as he took guard and looked around him. Four slips, a gully, silly mid-off, silly mid-on, leg-slip and a square-leg, all crouching with eyes unnaturally bright. The capillaries popped in their cheeks, the veins throbbed in their temples. Lord Christie, whose figures stood at 6 for 17 after ten high-speed overs, ignored the silver flecks that danced before his eyes as he walked back to bowl.

Alan Tremoyne had decided to have a tonk. He might as well. He wasn't really a batsman. Nobody expected him to score the 198 necessary for victory. So, at what he judged the appropriate moment, he shut his eyes and carved the air massively with his bat. The ball shot straight up in the air, followed by the gleaming eyes of the fielders. This was it. It would be caught. They had won. It was falling towards Sir Alec Hogdirt at square leg. "Yours, Alec!" cried one of the fielders. "*Sir* Alec!" shouted Sir Alec, but didn't take his eyes from the red ball descending towards him. It was getting bigger. It was very red indeed, and huge. The whole sky was red and flaming. Why was somebody pulling a piano wire tight around his chest? Why were they hitting the backs of his legs with hammers? As Sir Alec pitched forward the ball hit him in the small of the back and bounced away. One by one the entire City eleven rolled his eyes, clutched at his throat and fell. The Toilchard Regis team ran on to the field, and with commendable unself-consciousness began giving their prone opponents the kiss of life. The Toilchard Regis wives ran on to the field as well, with the remains of the tea and a plate of headless gingerbread men.

The two German tourists, who had thought they were just getting the hang of it, looked at the eleven flanelled couples kissing on the ground and reflected that cricket was indeed a game hard to understand. But they took a photograph of it anyway.

THE LATIN LOOFAH

YOU HEAR A LOT as a bath attendant. HORACE D. STRIGIL had heard most of it. And he'd met them all. They'd all been in. Labienus, Cotta, Balbus. Even one or two from the third declension. They all came to his bath. You could steam anywhere. But only at Horace's did you get the special extra. The Romans having been steamed, Horace Demetrius Strigil scraped them with his special thing. They'd name it after him—the Strigil. They steamed themselves in order to bring the dirt to the surface. Then Horace got at them with the Strigil.

The other bath operators had tried to get the secret from him. They had attacked him with spears, weapons and arrows. But they hadn't got it off him. Only Horace could make a Strigil that got rid of the understains.

He thrived. He had thrived. He was thriving. Would that he would thrive for many days, months and years. The Imperial family's patronage had been better than a poke in the eye with a blunt spear, sword or dart. Tiberius had come in first, then Claudius. Nearly died, Claudius had—caught a chill trying to ask for more hot water. Then Caligula had been in. Rum chap, Caligula. His horse had made a terrible mess of the rowing machine. Not as bad as Nero, though. Nero had been in for the first time today, and had obviously taken a fancy to Horace. He had asked one of those questions expecting the answer yes. Horace had declined to be conjugated. Nero had left in a huff. Horace having turned Nero down, he hoped there wouldn't be trouble.

Thoughtfully, he stropped another Strigil. He wasn't sure, but he thought he could smell burning.

THE PRESENTERS

(Barry Norman)

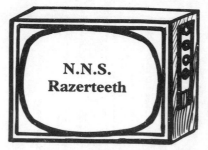

(Esther Rantzen)

(Reginald Bosanquet)

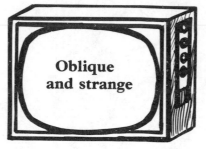

(Reginald Bosanquet)

(Michael Parkinson)

(David Coleman)

ALEC R. SHOTRIGID

They sent Bulstrode to the station in the Simms-Welbeck to meet him and bring him back to Graveningham. Twice before, on grey autumn days like this, Bulstrode had made the journey: Sir Borthwick returning from the Crimea, and young Mortimer from the Boer War. But then Bulstrode had only been a footman, and had ridden on the back of the Shotrigids' coach. Now he was a chauffeur, and drove the Shotrigids' Simms-Welbeck landaulette. It was 1917. He must hurry—the London train was due at twenty past.

On the return journey, he kept glancing in his rear-view looking-glass at the pale figure on the buttoned back seat. Alexander Rainham Shotrigid—young Master Alec that had been so keen to go to the war, as all Shotrigids went to the war. But Bulstrode had never seen one come back like this. The Somme, they said he'd been to. Bulstrode had looked for it on the map in the library one evening while Sir Borthwick was having dinner. Abroad, it was. It had obviously done Master Alec no good.

Alec, by a superhuman effort, managed to bring to mind every servant's name as he went along the line. Seventy-three handshakes later, Nanny led him into the house, through the hall with its husks of armour and weaponed walls and left him by the drawing-room door. She patted him on the shoulder. "There's Nanny's brave little soldier, then. You go in and see your father, and stop blinking like that, Master Alec, it doesn't do."

Sir Borthwick possibly had the best intentions in synchronising the opening of the champagne with Alec's entry into the drawing room. As he saw the handle turn, he signalled to Baring, the butler, whose thumbs began their irresistible upward thrust.

Alec, blinded by the setting sun through the tall west windows, saw nothing. But he heard the pop. His hands went to his ears, and

'*The Somme, they said he'd been to. It had obviously done Master Alec no good.*'

he threw himself behind the sofa, shouting wildly, "No more. Not tonight. Can't they wait? Aren't they satisfied? Wasn't Tomkins enough? He's out there, Sergeant! Tomkins! And Smither. Sergeant! Wake up! Oh, God, they've got the Sergeant! Corporal, they've got the Sergeant! Oh, God, they've got the Corporal! No more! No more noise! Let Tomkins sleep. Let us all sleep!"

His father looked down at him. "Have you quite finished, sir? Is that all you're going to do for us tonight?" He dismissed the butler with a nod. Baring backed out of the door. Sir Borthwick turned to his son again. "I don't think I have ever seen a more embarrassed servant. How could you behave like that in front of him? Now get up and pull yourself together." Alec rose to his feet, and stood in front of his father. His left arm would not stop shaking and he blinked continuously. "Now," said his father, "we have gone to some trouble to see that you enjoy yourself during your leave, so I hope we're not going to see any more of that sort of carrying on. There'll be a shoot for the next three days, then fireworks. And champagne every night—the 87's about ready and getting gassier by the day, so we might as well let it throw its cork at you as at anyone. But no more of that shoutin', mind."

★ ★ ★

Bulstrode marvelled at the change as he drove Master Alec to the station. Only home an hour, and he looked like a new man. He hoped Sir Borthwick wouldn't mind; he wasn't sure Sir Borthwick knew that Master Alec was going back to the war.

"Goodbye, Bulstrode," said Alex, his eyes unnaturally, almost feverishly bright. "And don't tell the pater I've gone. He'll find out in a couple of days anyway."

"Goodbye, Master Alec," said Bulstrode. "Back to the war, then?"

"I certainly am, Bulstrode. Bit of peace and quiet, what?"

NO BLOOD ON THE SAND

When CARLOS GRITHIDE waves to all the crowd at his
　　bullfights,
They notice that he doesn't sport the normal suit of lights.
He wears a sort of babygro of asphalt mixed with gravel
And enters to the rhythms of the Bolero by Ravel.
Maybe this circumspection earns him rather less applause
But his Life Insurance costs less than the other matadors'.

GROCER TALDISHI

IT WAS WITH considerable pride that Sarfraz Taldishi looked round his shop. What stocks! What range! What neat and attractive display shelves, what hygienic wipe-clean surfaces, and how clean all of them had been wiped! The freezer cabinet's sharp straight lines were unrounded by ice build-up, the cash register stood ready to write out green electronic numbers while whistling like a miserly bird.

Sarfraz Taldishi was proud all right. But not just proud. Worried. Worried and tired. Staying open seven days a week made you tired. Staying open twenty-four hours a day, seven days a week made you even more tired. He supposed it would be easier when Mushtaq was older. But Mushtaq must finish school. He was a good boy, Mushtaq. His mother had done well with him. Sarfraz sometimes wished she had not done quite so well, and that Mushtaq had not turned out so clever. Then maybe he would do less homework and be more help in the shop. But it was how it was, and that was how it should be.

It was more than Mushtaq's success at school that worried Sarfraz Taldishi. It was business. He could not understand why business was so bad. He looked round the shop again. It was arranged just the way his friend Ghupte had told him. Ghupte had explained, on his last visit, all about cash flow, point of sale, display material, and staying open twenty-four hours a day, seven days a week. This was how Ghupte ran his shop. While other shops went to the wall (that had been his phrase, his very words— went to the wall), Ghupte prospered. He offered, he said, a service that no supermarket could offer. At any hour of any day, the customer could buy from him. And buy they did. Not the whole week's shopping, perhaps, but the extra bits and pieces. Enough to make Ghupte a prominent person, he said, a member of the Willesden Junior Chamber of Commerce. He had been approached to join the local branch of the Lions Club. "You ought

to know more about lions than most of us," one of their members had said, and Ghupte, who had never seen a lion or been to Africa, had smiled and assumed it to be another English joke.

Ghupte had told Sarfraz Taldishi all this when he had visited him. Sarfraz had listened, impressed, and when Ghupte left had altered his entire shop to make it as much like Ghupte's description of his own as it was possible to make it. Out went the bins of rice, the boxes of lentils. In came Nescafe, Kleenex (and Delsey and Andrex), aspirin, chocolate biscuits, vol-au-vent cases and frozen pizza. And yet it hadn't worked. No-one who came into his shop ever bought anything. In two weeks he had sold a box of matches and a packet of wire wool. The ham was beginning to smell, and the paté seemed to have more black bits in it than before. Perhaps he should go to Willesden like his friend Ghupte. He was certainly getting nowhere here in Pakistan.

BY OUR MOTORING CORRESPONDENT

HELLO THERE, KNIGHTS of the road. ERIC ROADLIGHTS here, with more glad tidings for those of you who don't feel dressed without the car-coat and the gloves with holes in the back. This week I've been testing a brand-new product under the gruelling motoring conditions provided by the roads of Bermuda. The SR lubricants people chose this sun-soaked paradise to launch a new line which could revolutionise car-care.

Ever felt that your upholstery lets down the rest of the car? The bodywork shines (SR waxes can help here) the chrome sparkles (SR Chromopol is one of the many excellent brands on the market) but the old leather just isn't up to it. Of course, nancy-boys with cloth upholstery can stop reading now—this one's for real drivers in a real leather driving seat. And for those real drivers the good news is that SR GT CAR HIDE OIL is the product you've been waiting for. Applied three or four times daily, it can make that cracked old leather shine like new.

Of course, there'll be the moaning Minnies who say that it makes the seats slippery. And I have to admit that, taking the Bermudan hairpins with bags of loud pedal, you could sometimes end up in your passenger's lap. Which, with the passenger SR provided for me, was no great hardship—I wouldn't say she was supple, but could you limbo under a Maserati Bora? And if the wailing Willies don't like sliding about, they can always wear the old scaredy-straps.

The grousing Gordons may say that SR GT Car-Hide Oil comes off on your trousers. I wouldn't know. With the hospitality SR and their charming hostesses showed us I never got a chance to get the old trousers on! But anyway, to the complaining Conrads I say: a bit of oil on the trousers tells the world that you're a man with leather seats in his car, and that can't be bad!

No, I think you can rely on my reputation as a pretty hard chap to convince when I say that, after three weeks testing this stuff in pretty tough sub-tropical conditions here in Bermuda (and a special word to congratulate the local airline, ReggAer, who brought us out here, on the service—and the stewardesses!), I reckon SR GT Car-Hide Oil is a must for anybody who puts his car first.

See you in next week's column, knights of the road, and keep those dice dangling!

Eric Roadlights

Note to Advertising Manager

I've shown this to SR and they say
it's OK and they'll be in touch. They
were talking in terms of a whole page
- not bad, eh! It might be worth
bending ReggAer's elbow on the strength
of the reference to them. Not that
they deserve it. We were bloody lucky
to get home the way the pilot drank.
I enclose two cleaning bills for the
suits which got oily.

E.R.

CALL
SLIP

MON | TUE | WED | THUR | FX | SAT

Thank you for your order.
Please bring this ticket when
collecting articles.

CA
SLI

MON | TU

Thank y   t when
Please bri
collecting   cles.

IRISH GEAR CO. LTD

"WE WANT YOU to design us some civilian clothes there," said the man in the dark glasses and the beret, gesturing in a far from civilian way with his M-16 carbine, "but they all have to be identical. So that they look smart on marches, if we happen to go on any marches. My card there." He handed over a small, nearly rectangular segment of pasteboard on which were typed the words "I.R.A. CHRIST LODGE, 79d Falls Road, Belfast." "We're the religious wing of the I.R.A.," he added helpfully.

"Had you anything particular in mind?" asked SCOT HAIRGIRDLE, who had seen many things in Belfast, but never a full-blooded Provo with a clothing order.

"We are true Irishmen. We have absolutely nothing in mind. You make clothes. We make war," said the civilian soldier fiercely. "I'll be after calling back after two weeks there." And he turned on his heel, regained his balance and marched out. Seconds later he came back in. "The measurements is on the back of the card. There's four of each. Seventeen in all, with the rabbit." Again he slammed the door. Again it re-opened almost immediately. "The rabbit," he said "is quite big and is 7 inside leg front and 9 inside leg back. He can't manage buttons." This time the exit was final.

Scot Hairgirdle, his hands shaking a little, carried the piece of pasteboard into the workroom. He tucked it into a pocket of his blouson and clapped his hands for attention. The sewing machines slowed to a silence. "Children," said Scot, "I have news for you. From tomorrow denim is out!"

The three ladies at their sewing machines clapped happily. This, they had found, usually kept the boss happy. The boss smiled briefly, then continued, "From today, however, my darlings, denim is still in, and I don't recall telling you to stop." He flounced out of the workroom, and through the lobby, pushing

100

'The police were there to see fair play, the
army was there because it had been told to be, the
Irish Gear Co. Ltd was there to see its uniforms and
the Rev. Ian Paisley was there to be seen by all the others.'

open the door marked "Design".

Thanks to Scot Hairgirdle, the IRISH GEAR CO. LTD had survived the troubles. Churning out jeans, waistcoats, shirts and caps in denim, they had scraped through, with the occasional order for a coat and skirt for the inauguration of another doomed building providing a little jam on top of the scrape. Scot looked through the one-way mirror at his work force bent over their sewing—DORIS LACERIGHT, HILDA CORSETRIG and ERICA GOLDSHIRT: Prod, Papist and Jew respectively, working amiably if not happily on the blue sea of denim. He turned to his associates. "Who's just got an order for seventeen outfits?" he asked, and studied the nail on his middle finger as if it were a hand mirror. From their drawing boards, ARCHIE GIRLDOTS and CHRISTAGEL DIOR looked up, a bit interested. They became more interested as Scot explained the requirements of the I.R.A. Christ Lodge.

★ ★ ★

Scot, Archie, Christagel, Hilda, Doris and Erica did not normally go up the Shankill. Or the Falls. Or Andersontown. It was safer to stay in the parts that mixed. But today they stood, coney coats tight-buttoned against the bitter cold, waiting for their uniforms to march down the street. The police stood by them. The army stood by them. None of them could see much because the Rev. Ian Paisley stood in front of them. All of them were there because they had been told (by a press release delivered by hand to the *Belfast Telegraph*) that the I.R.A. Christ Lodge would march down the Shankill Road in uniform, through the heart of Protestant territory. The police were there to see fair play, the army was there because it had been told to be, the Irish Gear Co. Ltd was there to see its uniforms on display and the Rev. Ian Paisley was there to be seen by all the others.

They could hear cheering now, and laughter from further up the road. Scot nudged Archie, and smiled. The cheering and the laughter grew to a peak as the sixteen I.R.A. men and their rabbit marched past in the uniforms Scot had designed for them. Nobody threw anything. Nobody shot anyone. Everybody except the I.R.A. laughed. And Scot thought how nice his clients looked in their orange bomber jackets.

ERICA THIRL'S DOG

MY NOSE IS wet and shiny, and I never clean my teeth,
Sometimes I lie upon my back and show my underneath,
I do things on the pavement when I'm taken to the shops,
And instead of being punished, I am given chocolate drops.
My name is "Sit", I think, although it might be "Fetch" or
      "Stay",
But whatever people call me I come running anyway,
And I live with Mrs Thirl in quiet South Coastal widowhood,
And we walk and talk together while she throws me bits of
      wood.

Sometimes she thinks that I can understand each single word;
I can't. That's why I never find her chattering absurd.
I cannot reason, cannot laugh, I cannot count to ten;
I count one, and then more-than-one, then more-than-one
      again.
Yet people in their more-than-ones to pets like me will turn
For friendship and companionship—both words I cannot
      learn—
For my conditioned reflexes are just designed to fill
The gap that's left by humans when they're absent, cross or ill.

I never see why I'm considered Mrs Thirl's best friend,
Until her daughter Lynne brings all her brood for the weekend.
Then Mrs Thirl from dawn to dusk makes orange juice and
      cake,
And Lynne says she stays with Don only for the children's
      sake.
And Mrs Thirl says, "Darling, your Dad was just the same.

Children, run out in the garden, Gran's too busy for a game."
Then Lynne goes boo-hoo-hoo and says that next time will be
    final,
And as they cry I lick their salty tears from off the vinyl.

My life's not complicated like the humans she adores,
I don't complain of migraine, or go through the dogopause,
I don't forget to thank her for my birthday postal order,
I never kick my football into her herbaceous border.
I cannot help but wag my tail and pant apparent thanks
(I've no alternative—I'm thick as more-than-one short planks),
But my wagging, and my panting, and my dying-for-the-queen
Is the nearest thing to true love Mrs Thirl has ever seen.

THE OLYMPIC IDEAL

HE STOOD ON one leg and shook the other. He ran gently on the spot. It was cold and very high. HOTLEGS RICARDI, the Italians' white hope for the 1500 metres, looked round the Andorra Olympic stadium. Behind him the band played "God Save the Queen" as another British hope mounted the winner's rostrum. Across the stadium he saw a Russian lady shot-putter zipping up her flies as she emerged from the Gents.

Andorra had not wanted the Olympic games, but as the only country who had offended nobody at all for a decade or more, it was inevitable that Andorra would get the Olympic games. In a desperate attempt to avoid the crippling cost, Andorra tried to gain the world's disapproval by invading Spain. At the orders of the Andorran government the Andorran army marched across the border in broad daylight. But when after three days of occupying Spain even the local Spanish papers had made no mention of its presence, the army went back to Andorra and apologised to the Andorran government, who said it was all right and he had done his best and he could go home now. So the Andorran army went home and started to draw up plans for the stadium, because he was also the Minister of Works.

The games had gone quite well, considering, apart from the marathon. Andorra was not big enough to hold the whole marathon course, which had had to include a loop into France and back. France had been very unco-operative about this, and the marathon times had as a result been very disappointing—as indeed they were bound to be in a race containing two passport checks and a body-search. The 1500 metres was safe within the stadium, though, and hopes of a new world record were high. They rested mainly on the man who stood shaking his arms and legs in the chill mountain air. The world's sports fans had taken to their hearts Hotlegs Ricardi, a child of the slums of Naples, and a gift for the sub-editor because he read meters.

He worked for the Neapolitan Electricity company, and trained as he made his rounds. Down the basement stairs he ran, through the passages that smelt of oil, past the dumpy ladies in their black dresses, past the pasta hanging on the chair to dry, raise the torch, read the meter, make a note, run back up the basement stairs, run next door, into the church door, crossing himself, run down into the crypt, past the strange plastic limbs put there to remind the Almighty which bits of his flock needed attention (Mamma Ricardi had put two legs in the cabinet last week to make sure the Father ran by his side in the race), into the cupboard beside the crypt, raise the torch, read the figures, write them down, keep running on the spot, running, running. The British papers said he trained for the 1500 metres by doing 120 meters a day. He did not understand the British press. But they showed a picture of him in his running clothes writing down the meter reading at the Napoli stadium. He had only once run at the Napoli stadium, once. Against the clock. Three minutes twenty-nine seconds, they had said. He did not know whether that was fast. They said it was. Today he would find out. Today he ran not against the clock, but against other men, in the Olympics. He had never done this before. There had not been time. They had not let him. Six days he read his meters and ran through Naples. The seventh day was Mass and looking after Mamma. Today he would find out if he was a fast runner, or just a meter-reader from Naples.

The others were taking off their track-suits now. He removed the donkey jacket and threw it aside, the legend "Electricita Napolitana" gleaming orange on its back. They lined up. The men in the camel-hair coats who trained the team had told him to let the others lead. He had the big sprint finish, they said. Stay behind the others, stay out of trouble. Then on the third lap. . .!

The gun surprised him, and he found he had no choice but to obey their orders. He *was* behind the others, but only a little, and it was easy to keep up. They did not, he thought, go very fast. He ran steadily, maybe five metres behind the pack, watching their numbered backs moving up and down.

After one lap he still felt fine.

After two laps he was bored. This was very easy. He had no need to worry. The pack ran on in front.

At the beginning of the final lap they rang a bell, a bell just like a doorbell, the sort of doorbell he rang all day. Why did they ring the bell? What was he doing here? He was running. The 1500 metres. He would never manage 1500 meters. He must hurry. Not pausing for a second, Hotlegs Ricardi made his decision; he stopped, grabbed a clipboard from a track official and calmly copied down all the numbers from the backs of the disappearing runners.

Politics

ELECT	VOTE	JOIN
That grim E.E.C. hag (Maggie Thatcher)	**Wet hardhead** (Edward Heath)	**Joky Sinner** (Roy Jenkins)

Son-of-Politics

Len Verbdrain
(Bernard Levin)

I'M A LITTLE STIFF FROM BADMINTON

AT BADMINTON they met, and there their romance had
     its birth,
As she admired his snaffle, and he ogled at her girth;
For she was OLGA DITCHRISER, the reigning British champ,
And he was CARL HORSEDIGIT from the rival German camp.
Together at the horse trials they galloped through the wood,
And got off with each other in a way no rider should,
But by the time that Burghley came around, their love was
     spent
And people said, "We knew it was a mere three-day event."

HOLLYWOOD GRATES

by
Bryan Marron

Transcript of Episode 34, requested by GERARD H. SOLICIT, attorney-at-law, representing the estate and relict of OSCAR LIGHTRIDE (dec.).

The programme was recorded in Los Angeles during 1981 immediately following the death of Oscar Lightride. Bryan Marron acted as director and presenter of the series, interviewing various survivors of the film industry's golden years.

TITLE SEQUENCE

Montage of old film stars by their firesides. Super-impose title, "HOLLYWOOD GRATES". Zoom in on flames. Super-impose "OSCAR LIGHTRIDE". Pan across to Bryan in chair. "INTRODUCED BY BRYAN MARRON".

Bryan: Hollywood is not a place noted for its loyalty. You trust the person on your left at your peril. Indeed, you could say that the anti-trust laws were introduced just to stop the Beverly Hills from letting each other down. Indeed they say that, if you really want to surprise someone here, you stab them in the front! Indeed, as the gossip writer OLGA DIRTRICHES has said, "Loyalty in Hollywood is about as common as prawns at a bar-mitzvah," and it's not impossible to agree with her. But one person for whom Hollywood did feel loyalty was Oscar Lightride, who died earlier this year at the age of seventy. I asked the director, Henry Sigal, whether he thought Oscar Lightride was a great actor.

H. SIGAL (DIRECTOR):   A great actor? No! A good actor?
No! But a star? Ah, well—definitely not! Oscar was—well,
he was one of those guys who—well, who keep a film unit
together. He listened to people. He made sure everyone
had a chair. He drove people home. A nice guy, you know?

Bryan: A nice guy. (Pause.) In many of the movies with
which Lightride was associated, the director of
photography was the remarkable camerawoman, ROSIE D.
ARCLIGHT. How does she remember him?

Rosie D. Arclight: Very vaguely. He was a nice enough
guy. No great features. Not much expression. But he could
hit his mark and say his line and didn't knock over the
furniture. Sigal kept him around out of guilt mainly, because
of Scarlet. I don't think Oscar ever knew about Scarlet
and Sigal. He wouldn't have guessed. He was—well, not
very— er—imaginative. Ask anyone. Ask his agent, SIGI L.
ACTORHERD.

Sigi L. Actorherd: Listen, you don't get to be somebody's
agent for forty years and not get to know them pretty well. I
guess I knew Arthur Lightside as well as any man living. You
know what I called him? Mister Nice Guy. You know what
he did? He sacrificed his career. That's what he did. He
sacrificed his career for Scarlet. She went out to the parties,
he stayed in, looked after the babies. Two of them. Little
Chinese kids. He adopted them. It was a good thing he didn't
go to the parties. He might have found out about Scarlet and
Rosie Arclight. That would've hurt him.

Bryan: The sort of places Scarlet would go to in the
evenings were the REARLIGHT DISCO, here in Sunset
Boulevard. I asked ROD GAELICSHIRT, international rock
superstar and habitué of the Rearlight Disco, what his
memories of Oscar Lightride were.

Rod Gaelicshirt: Was he the guy who was married to Scarlet? Christ, yes, I met him. I don't think he ever knew about us, though. She'd come here most nights, and sometimes she'd let me watch her and Rosie in the jacuzzi. Occasionally Sigal and I would get in there as well and, oh God that was funny—we were all well flying and she nearly drowned. That was the time I met him. The manager made him come and take her home. He turned up with these two Chinky children in their dressing-gowns at four a.m. Was he what? Was he any good as an actor? I didn't know he was an actor! Great!

Bryan: Oscar Lightride appeared in many films, usually those starring his wife. The roles for which he is most remembered are probably those in CIRO'S DEATHGIRL, in which he played Man in bus queue, and ORICA'S THIRD LEG, in which he was Second man in pet shop. Both films were produced by the veteran Rumanian, SHLOD GERIATRIC.

Shlod Geriatric: You vant know sumsink about moviss? You vant know vot der most important part in a movie iss? I tell you. Most important part in a movie iss Second men in pet shop. You know vie? I tell you. Identification. Der public dey don't identify mit der stars! Dey identify mit Second men in pet shop. So Second men in pet shop got to be ordinary schmo. Diss vas Oscar. He vas best ordinary schmo in der business. But der vife! Oi! You meet der vife! Vot a Kobbelcracker she vass! You know how old I am? Vell, how old do I look? Eighty-five? Eighty-eight? Exactly. I'm thirty-eight. Det is vot she could do to a men.

GERI O'CHILDSTAR: I acted with Oscar, and not many people can say that. He didn't really, well, act as such. He just sort of was. I was *First* man in pet shop in *Orica's Third Leg.* I guess I got the plum role because of all those years with Lassie. I mean, I couldn't say I've had the same sort of

success as a mature actor as I'd enjoyed as a boy, but I still have a certain standing in this business. Oscar? No, not even nominated. It wasn't that sort of. . . oh—that Oscar! Sorry—yes. He was great; really supportive. And sweet the way he'd go and chat to Wang and Foo in between takes. I don't think he ever resented other people's success. I'm not sure that he wouldn't have found First man in pet shop too much to handle. It had three lines. And a puzzled frown. He wasn't the jealous type. Though if he'd known about Scarlet and me. . .

SOL E. THIRDCIGAR: Mr Marron, I'm a busy man and I didn't get to be head of a major motion picture chain without speaking my mind. As they say in France, cherchez la femme. You know what that means, Mr Marron? You do? You French? You're not. Don't tell me. It means find the broad, Mr Marron. And to find the broad in Oscar Lightride's case, you look under almost anyone in Hollywood. SCARLET O'HIDRIG is a big star, Mr Marron, and people treat her like a star: they land on her looking for signs of human life. She gave Oscar the runaround, Mr Marron. Wang and Foo, too. They were good kids. For twenty years she did nothing for them. They must be—oh, twenty-three, twenty-four now. Really cut up about Oscar's death. Why am I telling you this, Mr Marron? Because I liked Oscar, and I'd promised him a picture. It was a film about a pet shop owner. Nice part. He was going to play the lead. He was a warm guy. He would have been good. He went home and told Scarlet. The next morning they find him dead and everyone says it's suicide because he never made it. Now he knows and I know and now you know that he had made it and I know that his wife was on the slide and she knew that and you're a clever man, Mr Marron, you know French, you work it out for yourself. Have a nice day.

Scarlet O'Hidrig: Why, Mr Marron, why's a big boy like you asking questions like that? Now you just come and sit over here next to little Scarlet, and I'll show you how we fake those love scenes. You film journalists just love to get right inside the business, don't you? And since Oscar died, I. . .

[*Transcriber's Note.*   At this point, it is hard to see exactly what happens because the camera is knocked violently to one side, but it appears that two young Chinamen run into the room and attack the lady on the sofa. Mr Marron appears in shot and seems to be shouting "Hang in there, Wang and Foo." The two Chinamen then jump out of the window, which is closed, and the apartment was quite high up because a plane went past earlier in the interview (I think a bit of another film must have got edited on at the end). Mrs Lightride is lying very still at the end. Then the camera stops and the screen goes blank. I hope this makes sense.]

PRAY†TV

CHARLIE GODSTIR'S on his knees,
Praying to his Lord above:
"Lord, make people watch me, please,
So that millions know your love.
Make them switch on their TV's
So that millions know your grace -
Then we can put up the fees
For the advertising space."

ICH BIN EIN DUBLINER

AS THE CITROËN PRESTIGE turned out of the Elysée gates into the Faubourg St Honoré, the white-gloved hands of the palace guard flashed in salute. The motorcycle outriders turned right into the rue de Miromesnil, past the Ministry of the Interior. The car followed them smoothly, as if being towed by a silent tractor, when they turned again into the rue La Boëtie. In the back seat, GISCARD O'HITLER, France's new President, waved graciously to the occasional passer-by. He sat back, his legs barely reaching the thick carpet, and reflected yet again how easy it had been.

They passed the Cercle Militaire and continued up the rue de Vienne. "Ah Wien," thought the President. But that was long ago. Before Germany. Before Ireland. He put down his copy of *Le Monde*. A good name for a newspaper. He would keep it. Tomorrow, he would tell the Minister of the Interior to put the daily press under state control. The magazines had already been dealt with. Today, *L'Europe*—tomorrow, *Le Monde*. It was all so easy.

Not getting out of the bunker. That hadn't been easy. He had been stuck in the bunker for what seemed like days. Mind you, his golf had improved since then. He had reached Ireland easily, unnoticed and unrecognised. Of course, the moustache had had to go. That had been quite a wrench. It would have hurt less if he'd used a razor. He had got a job in Cork, within hours of getting off the boat. The Irish needed house-painters like anyone else. He had added the 'O' to his name on arriving in Ireland. The man at the registrar's office had said there were no forms to fill in. To add an 'O' was to add nothing, and if you add nothing, everything stays the same. So why fill in a form?

His next move had been into politics. So easy—as always, find
the enemy within and exploit him. Of whom were the Irish
frightened? Why, of the little people. Only in the last year had
their primeval fear subsided enough for them to elect their first
leprechaun Prime Minister. But SIR GERALD O'TICH had a shaky
power-base. O'Hitler's speeches insinuated that all Ireland's ills
were due to Sir Gerald O'Tich and the little people. "What
Rainbow? What Crock of Gold?" he would scream from the
rostrum. And during the night, his greenshirts moved through the
town, stealing washing and turning the milk sour. Eventually,
overwhelming public support forced the greenshirts into power
and kept them there. For O'Hitler had German scientists brought
from America to revolutionise Irish industry. Within weeks, they
had developed a remarkable fuel made from the herbs which grow
profusely in Ireland. The country's dependence on oil from
abroad was gone—home-grown herbs could supply her with
abundant cheap energy. "Whatever you think of O'Hitler," said
the Irish, "at least he made the trains run on thyme!"

From then it had been plain sailing. There had been embarrassing moments of course. The hand sometimes paused, rigidly, before waving to the crowds. The Israeli Prime Minister's visit had been marred by that unfortunate incident. And there had been confusion when O'Hitler began his victory speech with the words, "Ich bin ein Dubliner." But the press department had explained everything. Where was the point of equipping and arming a press department, if they couldn't then explain things?

They were now in the Avenue de Clichy. The day seemed quiet. France, if anything, had been easier than Ireland. Every Friday he had left the buoyant and booming Ireland and flown to Toulouse, where by wearing a camel-hair coat over his tracksuit he rapidly became the manager of the local football team. Under his eye, Toulouse had a wonderfully successful season—largely because just before the match he would say to the opposing team manager, "Remind your team who they are playing. It makes for a better game." And the manager would turn to his footballers and say, "Remember—this afternoon we play Toulouse." So his team obediently played to lose and Toulouse won.

In no time Giscard O'Hitler (he had added the Giscard and had also grown another moustache) was manager of the French National Team, and another part of his scheme was complete. Every nation the French hate plays soccer—the English, the Germans, the Italians, the Dutch. And France almost always loses to them, her national passion being rugby (as well as what they refer to as "un morceau de l'autre"). Giscard O'Hitler reasoned that if, suddenly out of the blue, a French soccer team arrived capable of beating the age-old rivals, its manager might be a very popular person. So, having provided himself with enough funds (by the simple expedient of selling ten Claudes, three Delacroix and a Raphael which happened to be sitting in a Swiss bank vault with a number only he knew), he purchased the best players from the various national teams of the rivals: a German sweeper and goalkeeper, three English midfield providers, two Dutch wings and four Italian forwards. Within six months, fortified by the crowd's lusty singing of "Vous ne marcherez jamais seul", France had the World Cup, and Giscard O'Hitler was offered the presidency by a tearful government. (Tearful because, in times of national rejoicing in France, the riot police tend to get a little trigger-happy with the CS gas.)

He liked being President of France, he thought, as he turned out of the Avenue de St Ouen on to the ring road. He liked the Citroën Prestige, as well. Its bonnet had an uncircumcised look.

Already there were plans in both countries for his re-election. After he had been re-elected, he would make them go to the polls again—and again, until they were fed up with voting. One last election, he would promise them. To save yourselves this bother, why not elect me President for life? Then, when they found out, it would be too late. Democracy! Hah!

"Oui, monsieur?" said the chauffeur, and Giscard O'Hitler realised the "Hah!" must have been out loud. He remained silent.

"Nearly there, monsieur," said the chauffeur.

"Danke schön, begob," said O'Hitler, and cursed himself for his carelessness.

The Al autoroute does not go all the way to Calais yet. Even with a motorcycle escort, the N43 is still a slow road. At the outskirts of the port the Citroën turned left, leaving the glacier of 44-ton lorries heading for the Channel ferries. The chauffeur drove out along the N940 toward Cap Blanc Nez, and stopped the car by an opening in the stone wall. Giscard O'Hitler got out. He could hear the sea. Ordering the chauffeur to wait, he walked towards the sound.

Passing a derelict field shelter, he saw parked behind it the car from the Paraguayan embassy. There were three passengers in it. He raised his hand in salute, and the car gave three dull metallic thumps as three answering salutes hit the inside of its roof. The three passengers got out: one hugely fat, one tiny but with an unusually large head, and one who walked with the unmistakeable carriage of a soldier. They did not greet the French President but walked towards the edge of the cliff; he followed them, his overcoat thrown over his shoulders, its empty sleeves swinging in the sea breeze.

The four of them stood silently on top of the cliff at Cap Blanc Nez. From there, you could see England.

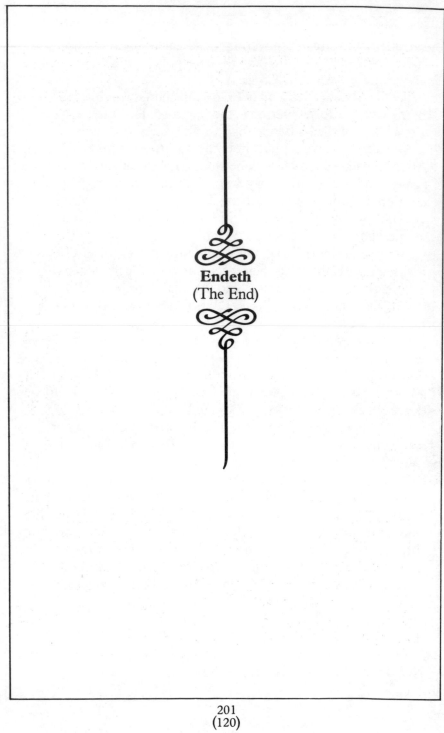

Endeth
(The End)